The German Opposition to Hitler

THE HUMANIST LIBRARY

Wheelwright & Regnery Co.
DISTRIBUTORS
23 East 26th Street,
New York 10, N. Y.

THE HUMANIST LIBRARY

The German Opposition to Hitler

AN APPRAISAL

by

HANS ROTHFELS

Professor of Modern History at the
University of Chicago

1948

Henry Regnery Company

HINSDALE, ILLINOIS

FOREWORD

THIS STUDY of the German "Resistance" goes back to a public lecture which was given at the University of Chicago on July 21, 1947. Though the study was never meant to be in any way exhaustive or to aim at a narrative of events, it is presented in a very considerably enlarged form, and with emphasis upon the less publicized parts of the story. The author also felt it his duty to add somewhat extensive notes, in order to point out all available evidence and to offer means of critical checking on controversial questions. Though facts of German opposition are abundantly known by now, their importance, their potential bearing upon contemporary issues and their meaning in a broader historical sense, still appear to be under a heavy cloud. It is to this interpretative side that the study is mainly devoted. And if it results in a "vindication," it is, in the author's opinion, not only one of considerable sections of the German people, but also and more basically one of the human spirit "*in extremis*." In a cycle of poems which one of the doomed conspirators against Hitler, Pastor Dietrich Bonhoeffer, wrote in prison, and which he called "Stations on the Road to Freedom," we read:

Not in following will, but in doing and daring of justice,
Not in possible deeds, but in real ones bravely attempted,
Not in the flight of thought, but only in Action, is Freedom.
Up and out of your hesitant fear into storms of occurrence,
Only supported by God's command and the faith that is in you!
Freedom then shall receive your spirit with jubilant welcome.[1]

---

[1] Translation by J. B. Leishman (*Time and Tide*, London).

THE author wishes to take this opportunity to thank those friends and colleagues who have generously supported him in assembling published and unpublished material. He is also greatly indebted to his assistant Mr. P. Wolfson.

CONTENTS

	PAGE
INTRODUCTION	9
Basic Aspects of Opposition.	9
Obstacles to Truth.	15
CONDITIONS AND POTENTIALITIES	23
German "Submissiveness"	23
Degrees of "Nonconformity"	27
Attitude toward Jews.	31
Intellectuals and Churches	34
PLANS AND ACTIONS	47
Early Nuclei	47
Crisis of 1938	58
Military Sector	63
Political Structure	85
Constitutional and Social Ideas	100
Kreisau Circle.	112
INTERNATIONAL ASPECTS	130
Peace Moves	130
"Unconditional Surrender"	149
SUMMARY	158
INDEX	167

INTRODUCTION

1

Basic Aspects of Opposition

Anyone who approaches the problems of the German opposition to Hitler will feel impelled to turn first to the most conspicuous evidence of Resistance, to the attempt on the Führer's life which occurred on July 20, 1944. Among a number of planned or miscarried actions, this was the one which actually materialized and came close to the goal. Thus, July 20 has gained something of a symbolic meaning. And whatever the shortcomings of the conspirators, technically or otherwise, whatever their "bad luck" or concurrence of adverse circumstances, the historian's foremost duty should be to pay tribute to the men who worked for the day of reckoning or stood ready for it, and to the many thousands who suffered and died for it. Only a few officers were shot on the spot or had an opportunity to take their own lives. Most of the victims went through months of "interrogation"—of nightly cross-examination, carried on under glaring lights and interrupted by direct torture. They had to face threats to their wives and children, threats which often enough were carried out. It is said to have been an accepted rule in the French Resistance that nobody was expected to withstand the various forms of Gestapo "conditioning" for more than twenty-four hours. If he was able to shield his associates that long, they might find a way of escape.

Measured by such a standard of more than average courage and endurance, the steadfastness of the men and women who were kept in the dreaded cellars of the Gestapo (Prinz-Albrechtstrasse), in dark closets too narrow to sit down in, or elsewhere in solitary confinement, stands out as a testimonial which is in itself of historic significance. It was not the attitude of a few only. About 7,000 persons were arrested, and according to an official source, "based on names and places," more than 4,980 were shot, hanged, or tortured to death in the reign of terror which followed July 20.[1] It is true: Some of them were forced to confess and some had nothing substantial to confess, because they were simply swept into the dragnet of a persecution which caught up with certain broad categories of "silent opponents" or settled old accounts. Yet it seems an established fact that, by the unbroken spirit of those who knew of at least one sector or another, the Gestapo was prevented from ever grasping the full extent of the conspiracy.[2] And a good many who fell as direct or indirect victims of the Twentieth of July stood the supreme test in a fashion which should make them memorable in the books of humanity, whatever the political implications of their plans or whatever light they shed upon the darkest phase of German history. The defendants in the trials appeared as accusers, rather than as accused criminals. They accepted martyrdom as an honor, as their contribution to "the brotherhood of man." And the consciousness of dying for a cause beyond their own lives did not waver at the threshold of an ignominious death. When the Jesuit, Father Delp, was led to the gallows, he said to the Catholic prison chaplain smilingly: "In a few minutes I shall know more than you."[3] Pölchau, the Lutheran chaplain in Tegel, and an active member of the opposition himself, wit-

[1] For the "four stages of torture," for the attitude of the prisoners, and other important observations, see Chap. XI in F. v. Schlabrendorff, *They Almost Killed Hitler* (New York, 1947). The number of arrested persons is found in a recently published "SS Bericht über den 20. Juli" (*Nordwestdeutsche Hefte*, 1947, 1/2, p. 33). This report also states that about 700 officers were executed. The quotation containing the figure on victims is taken from a press release of the British Admiralty, published on July 20, 1947, and based on captured German naval documents.

[2] Cf. H. B. Gisevius, *To the Bitter End* (Boston, 1947), p. 588. A confirmation of this (though only an indirect one) can be found in the SS report quoted in Note 1. It gives, in fact, a very incomplete analysis.

[3] P. Buchholz, who was a prison chaplain in Ploetzensee, gave a report of his experiences in *Neue Zeit*. Delp's words are quoted from "Der 20. Juli 1944," *Schriften des Südkurier* (Konstanz), p. 14. His letters, diaries, and meditations, written "between arrest and execution", have been published under the title, *Im Angesicht des Todes* (Frankfurt am Main, July, 1947). They contain some of the most remarkable documentations of the European spirit which came to life in the German Resistance.

nessed the same attitude of transcendence in the men to whom he administered.

From these few facts, a preliminary and very general conclusion may be drawn: No appraisal of the German opposition to Hitler can be adequate which keeps within the limited sphere of political considerations—that is, which inquires mainly into the oft-cited "class interests" or "national" aims of the conspirators—or takes its bearings from the external story of success or failure. Such so-called "realistic" interpretations are justified as far as they go. But in the last analysis we have to come down to fundamentals, to principles of moral affirmation beyond merely political exigencies. And we have to appreciate those spiritual forces of resistance which are not characteristic of the German scene alone, but by exceptional pressure were brought out in an exceptional way. Such was the interpretation which Count Moltke professed a few days before his execution. "So then," he wrote in his last letter to his wife,[4] "all that is left is a single idea, how Christianity can prove a sheet anchor in time of chaos."

While greatest emphasis should be placed on this basic aspect, it is necessary at the same time to broaden our view. Perhaps public attention has lately focussed too much on just one set of events and one set of victims. There are other examples of resistance which indicate a similar attitude on the part of the protagonists. We know enough today of the student revolt in Munich (February, 1943)[5] to

[4] Jan. 10, 1945. A translation of the letter was first published in *The Round Table*, June, 1946, pp. 224-30. It can now be found (together with the German original) in *A German of the Resistance, The last letters of Count Helmuth James von Moltke;* 2d edition, London, 1947. See also letter from Pölchau, chaplain of the Tegel prison, *ibid.*, pp. 69-70.

[5] See Rud. Pechel, *Deutscher Widerstand* (Zürich, 1947), pp. 96-102; Allen Welsh Dulles, *Germany's Underground* (New York, 1947), pp. 120-21; and more specifically, Karl Vossler, *Gedenkrede für die Opfer an der Universität München*, (München, 1947), and "Der 18. Februar, Umriss einer deutschen Widerstandsbewegung," *Die Gegenwart*, I, Nr. 20/21, Oct. 30, 1946. It is perhaps not quite accidental that the student revolt coincided with the completion of military preparations and with Schlabrendorff's attempt which will be discussed later on.

see in it more than the effect of the disaster at Stalingrad or of a specific provocation by the gauleiter of Bavaria. The Munich students Hans and Sophie Scholl had been fighting the party since their high school days; at the university, they were members of a group which carried on a pamphlet campaign (Letters of the "White Rose"). Connections existed between them and the Catholic periodical *Hochland*, with the Catholic writer Th. Haecker, with other universities, and probably with the active opposition, military and civilian. Yet the Munich students could hardly have believed that a spontaneous uprising would change the course of events. What they firmly believed in was the necessity of professing their faith and of purifying themselves as well as the name of Germany. "Is it not a fact," asked one of the leaflets, "that today every decent German is ashamed of his government?" Thus the manifesto of February 18, 1943, called upon the German youth "to avenge and to atone" so that they could contribute to "a new spiritual Europe." In the same vein, the sponsor of the group, Kurt Huber, a professor of philosophy, who shared the fate of execution with nine of its members, wrote in his last letter that death was to be the "fair copy" (*Reinschrift*) of his life. And on the walls of many houses in Munich appeared the inscription: "The spirit is alive."[6]

More realistic, one would suppose, was the plot which was hatched in Göring's Air Ministry in 1942. In contrast to most of the other movements, these plotters were in contact with the Soviets, and provided them with military information by a secret wireless. But the background of convictions and the awareness of a European mission were not fundamentally different. It was resistance on the basis of an ideally conceived communism. Of one of the leaders of the *Rote Kapelle*, Arvid Harnack, even the prosecuting attorney in the Air Ministry (known as "the bloodhound") said, "He died like a man."

[6] Vossler, *op. cit.*, p. 14. It is stated that the Letters of the White Rose continued to appear after the executions of July, 1943, and that remnants of the Scholl group, together with students at other universities, formed the cadres for the "Edelweiss" movement.

And Schulze-Boysen, another of the seventy-eight who were executed, wrote to his parents: "It seems a habit in Europe that spiritual seeds be drenched in blood."[7]

Besides these few very dramatic examples, there were innumerable others of courage, sacrifice, and martyrdom. Of course, not everybody who disappeared behind prison walls or barbed-wire fences, and not every deserter from the war, has a claim to be held up as a shining witness or a gallant hero. But the very fact that a considerable part of the Nazi apparatus was busy with keeping at least an equally considerable part of the German people in check or confinement, and that a full Nazi army was tied down by this task, cannot simply be left out of account. It is difficult to say how numerous were the German men and women, who before the war had already passed through or stayed in concentration camps. Estimates run from 750,000 to 1.2 millions,[8] and as to political prisoners included in this number, they run from 500,000 to 600,000.[9] The files of the Gestapo are said to

[7] Dulles, op. cit., p. 101. About Arvid Harnack and his American-born wife Mildred (who was sent to the gallows on "special order" of the Führer), see Axel v. Harnack (Gegenwart, January 31, 1947, pp. 15-18). The figure of 78 is given by Dulles; Ad. Grimme, in his article, "Widerstand vom Geist her" (which is dedicated to the memory of the poet Adam Kuckhoff) speaks of more than 400 members of the Rote Kapelle who were executed (Die Sammlung, II, 10).

[8] See They Fought Hitler First, published by the American Association for a Democratic Germany, with an introduction by W. E. Hocking (New York, 1945), p. 13. W. Ebenstein's estimate was that up to 1941, from one to one and a half million persons had passed in and out of concentration camps (The Nazi State, New York, 1943, p. 76). Ebenstein added that this was a "conservative" estimate; "other estimates run from two to two and one-half million" (loc. cit.). According to "Document R-129" (Nazi Conspiracy and Aggression, Washington, 1946, VIII, 198-202), there were, at the outbreak of war, 21,400 inmates in the six major camps; however, the total number of camps in existence at that time was 70 to 80 (Dulles, op. cit., p. 21), or even about 100 (E. Kogon, Der SS-Staat, Stockholm, 1947, p. 167). Hence the conclusions drawn from "Document R-129" by R. Brockwell (Central European Observer, 1946, p. 90), who tries to minimize the factor of political persecution, are very misleading.

[9] J. B. Jansen and St. Weyl, The Silent War, with a foreword by R. Niebuhr (Philadelphia and New York, 1943), p. 208. In October, 1946, 250,000 survivors were registered who had been persecuted for political reasons.

have contained the names of 2 million "suspect" persons; political death sentences up to 1938 are estimated at 12,000.[10]

These are some scattered items only. The files of the Gestapo have so far been used mainly for the purposes of the Nuremberg trials. It would be only fair to use them systematically for another purpose as well—namely, that of finding out what, in the eyes of the Gestapo, the attitude of the German people toward the Nazi regime actually was. Whatever the results of such an inquiry may turn out to be, no appraisal of the German opposition to Hitler can dispense with the broad significance of those figures on victims and suspects which are already known. Nor should we forget the nameless German workmen who carried on propaganda or committed sabotage, nor the political exiles who, at heavy risk, returned to underground work, nor the boys and girls of the "Edelweiss" groups or other "Packs" who fought the Hitler Youth. It is reported, for example, that in Krefeld, "at least 30 per cent of the Hitler Youth were secret Edelweiss members . . . the concentration camp at Neuwied (April, 1944) was reserved exclusively for teen-age boys." At a trial in 1939 a Gestapo agent testified that "at least 2 thousand boys and girls throughout the Reich" were organized in "The Pack."[11]

We should also take into account the intellectuals and artists of the so-called "Inner Emigration" who kept the lights burning (much better than outside observers imagined). Nor should we overlook the men and women who had courage enough to help their Jewish friends and neighbors, to hide and feed them, to provide them with forged papers or to arrange a sort of underground railway for persecuted persons. Of all this, evidence is available, and some deserves fuller discussion. But above all, it needs integration. In other words, a broad variety of facts has to be referred to the background

[10] These figures are quoted from W. Röpke, *Die deutsche Frage* (Zürich, 1945), p. 62 n. Some glimpses from the Gestapo files are given by G. A. Almond ("The German Resistance Movement," *Current History*, May-June, 1946).

[11] See the report of Ellen Marsh (*New Republic*, April 9, 1945); also *The Silent War*, pp. 255-59.

of conditions and potentialities as they existed in Germany. And more specifically, an attempt must be made to grasp the meaning of the German Resistance in its manifold forms, to describe its nature and extent, its component parts and its aims, its main lines of action inside as well as outside Germany. Only so can a certain balance sheet be prepared.

2

Obstacles to Truth

If such an attempt had been made three, or even two, years ago, it would have been little short of a provocation. At that time it was an almost universally accepted view in this country that there was not and never had been a German opposition to Hitler worth speaking of; that the Germans, differently from any other people and because of either inborn wickedness or an acquired habit of obedience or a specifically obnoxious political philosophy, voluntarily adhered or meekly submitted to a tyrannical regime of gangsters; that they deliberately closed their eyes to horrible crimes committed by Germans, and so on. According to this view it was only when the "Prussian generals" were faced with defeat that they started a movement to save their skins or to preserve the General Staff for World War III.

This misconception can be explained, in part, by objective difficulties which barred access to truth. A movement opposing a terroristic and thoroughly totalitarian regime[12] operates under conditions

[12] H. R. Trevor-Roper, in *The Last Days of Hitler* (New York, 1947), has taken pains to prove that "the Nazi state was not (in any significant use of the word) totalitarian" (p. 1), but rather, an ineffective Oriental sultanate. There is some truth in this. As an interesting article by Gerhard Ritter shows ("The German Professor in the Third Reich," *Review of Politics*, April, 1946), it was the very multiplicity of police and other controlling organs of party and state which offered certain loopholes. Nevertheless, no one can seriously deny the thoroughness of a terroristic system engulfing all aspects of life. Mr. Dulles, in his chapter on "The Evolution of a Police State," shows a much better grasp of this underlying reality than does the British Intelligence officer Trevor-Roper. His remarks on the German Resistance are misleading throughout the

which are unimaginable to anybody who has never lived in such a
"police state." To take a stand, to say nothing of a public stand,
was not only a matter of personal heroism (which seems a comparatively rare phenomenon in any modern society)[13] but also a
matter of gravely endangering one's family and one's friends.
It has been aptly said that Germany, after 1933, was "an occupied country,"[14] though in a very different sense than other
countries were to be. There was in Germany nothing of the glamor
which deservedly surrounds a "Resistance" fighting a foreign con-
queror and a tyrannical power imposed from outside. There prevailed instead, and particularly so in the later years, an atmosphere of
deadly silence, which probably deceived a good many Germans no
less than it deceived the public of Britain and the United States. Any
mentioning of names in clandestine propaganda or in broadcasts
abroad might have been disastrous. This danger, of course, increased
with the outbreak of war, which exposed any opposition to the
charge of high treason and forced the enemies of the regime to
detach themselves from "patriotic" interests, in the conventional
sense of the word. In addition, a constant shift of population and an
aerial bombardment which fell upon the just and the unjust alike,
could easily destroy existing cells of resistance and spread apathy.[15]
There were many reasons, then, for a deceptive picture of "all quiet."
And the German Intelligence and Counter Intelligence (*Abwehr*),

---

book. This hostile tendency comes to a climax with his almost regretful remark
(p. 45), that "of all the conquered countries of Europe, Germany alone produced no resistance movement"—that is, against armies of invasion and occupation!

[13] Even under the conditions of American society, it has often taken quite
some time for some courageous civilians to organize in opposition to the terror
of a local gangster regime.

[14] Dulles, *op. cit.*, p. 21.

[15] See the discussion of these effects by Dulles (pp. 168-69), "Instead of
gaining recruits, the anti-Nazis lost them," and by the United States Strategic
Bombing Survey, *Summary Reports*, 1945, p. 4, and *Over-all Report*, 1945, pp. 95,
108. To more detailed statements of the Bombing Survey, published in 1947,
reference will be made later on.

which was staffed with some of the most active members of the opposition, saw to it that this deceptive veil was kept as closely knit as possible. In particular, a "zone of silence" was drawn around the leading men of the conspiracy.

But this is not the whole story. It must be frankly stated that other than objective factors have a good deal to do with the misconception which was so widespread abroad. Some of these factors were of a broadly human nature, inasmuch as they derived from indifference or outright partiality. Of course, everybody was in a position to know that before the accession to power in January, 1933, the Nazis never polled more than 37 per cent of the vote (in July, 1932; in November, 1932, with economic conditions slightly improved, they polled 32 per cent), and that even after the burning of the Reichstag in the manipulated and hysterical elections of March, 1933, they reached only 44 per cent. But who among the general public outside Germany kept these facts in mind? It was well known, however, all over the world that, since early 1933, a wave of persecution had spread through Germany, and that the most energetic potential opponents were taken into so-called protective custody or had to flee the country. But as long as the inmates of concentration camps were Germans only, the horrors committed there were given little attention internationally. When the *Brown Book of the Hitler Terror* was published by Alfred Knopf in New York, it was reviewed in the *New York Times* of October 15, 1933, by Mr. James W. Gerard, former United States Ambassador to Germany.[16] With this very book before him, Mr. Gerard saw fit to write: "Hitler is doing much for Germany, his unification of the Germans, his destruction of communism, his training of the young, his creation of a Spartan state, animated by patriotism, his curbing of parliamentary government, so unsuited to the German character, his protection of the rights of private property are all good." When people who had fled Germany told their Eng-

[16] *New York Times*, October 15, 1933, Section V, pp. 1, 24. About Hitler himself, Mr. Gerard had this further to say: "No man who attains to great prominence escapes the suspicion of some form (!) of immorality."

lish or American friends about their own or their friends' experiences in Buchenwald or Oranienburg or Dachau, they often met with a mild incredulity, certainly with regard to the numbers involved or the methods applied.

Of course, all this changed in the spring of 1945. The unbelievable horrors which were then discovered in the liberated camps, as well as the unearthing of evidences of the crimes committed in Poland and Russia, shook the Western world. The actual findings proved worse than even the best-informed observers had expected. But when these proofs of German bestiality came to light, little was heard about the large number of Germans who had been among the victims. Victor Gollancz, the editor of the *Brown Book* (1933), writes in retrospect of "the outcry that deafened us at the time of the Buchenwald 'revelations,' which were no revelations at all to those who had been trying—ever since 1933—to rouse a lazy and sceptical public and to speak for men and women who ... were suffering unspeakable torments in those camps. ..." In fact, the obliviousness which he castigates was deliberately preserved. In no official report has the American public been told that there were practically no foreigners in Buchenwald until the summer of 1943, and that among the 20,000 survivors (51,000 having been killed), there were still 2,000 Germans of the Reich.[17] It would also be of interest to have statistical data about the composition of other German camps in 1945, data likely to be at the disposal of the Western Allies. Obviously the Gestapo was not of the opinion that all Germans were Nazis or, because of the war, were solidly behind the regime. It would also be of interest to know how many foreigners served in the special "death's-head" detach-

[17] *They Fought Hitler First*, p. 14. According to Kogon, an eyewitness of the Liberation (*op. cit.*, p. 358), the figures were 21,000 and 2,200, respectively. About the absence of foreign prisoners in Buchenwald (up to 1943), see Christopher Burney (*The Dungeon Democracy*, New York, 1946, p. 58). A pamphlet printed by the U. S. Seventh Army (*Dachau SS*) also states that, before the war, the number of foreign prisoners in Dachau was insignificant, and that during the war the Germans and Austrians became a numerical minority, the average number of Germans being about 3,000.—Quotation from Gollancz in: *Our Threatened Values* (Hinsdale, Ill., 1947), p. 41.

ments or in other units of the SS which were "in charge" of concentration camps.

Some scattered evidences are available which bear out the existence of such a "black international."[18] We know, for example, that among the guards at German camps, there were Croats and Ukrainians, and that "Protective Corps" were formed of Lithuanians, Latvians, and Esthonians who "took care" of their own conationals.

In the occupied countries, the same type was obviously picked for this assignment as in Germany. A great many native Dutchmen have been accused because they tortured their fellow Dutchmen, and in the Vichy camp in Gurs, which was French in administration, the death rate was hardly lower than in the "normal" German camps. A particularly striking evidence of this "international" comes from a Swiss witness who, on invitation of the French General de Lattre de Tassigny, took part in an inspection tour of southern Germany. He reported that the French in their zone of occupation also discovered a typical horror camp. But upon looking into the matter, they found that the guards, to a large extent, were French *miliciens*.[19] Of course, no information was ever given out about this camp. It would have contrasted too grossly with the official propaganda line. While all evidences and any sober examination would show that modern society creates within itself a dark reservoir—or rather, a sewer—the release of which means plain barbarism, and that there is potential material for torturers as well as for martyrs in every modern nation, a policy of hatred and revenge decided otherwise. In line with the Morgenthau plan and its underlying "Vansittartism," or with the supporting statement which General Eisenhower made in 1944 to the

[18] See the important chapter on the psychology of the SS in Kogon (*op. cit.*, pp. 359-75). Concerning Croats and Ukrainians, *ibid.*, p. 59. On the "Protective Corps," see *Nazi Conspiracy* (cf. Note 9), II, 226-27. It must also be mentioned that the "Waffen-SS" had a number of full-fledged foreign legions (see A. Vagts, *Journal of Politics*, August, 1947, pp. 406-7). On the other hand, since 1944 older German soldiers and even political prisoners were forced into SS uniforms and SS functions (see Joseph Joos, *Leben auf Widerruf*, Olten, 1946, p. 77).

[19] Quoted from Röpke, *op. cit.*, p. 224 n.

effect that the whole German population was "a synthetic paranoid,"[20] the thesis had to be maintained that there were no "good Germans" (except perhaps dead ones), and that bestiality was naturally a German preserve.

This leads to the core of the problem, as far as the obstacles to any correct appraisal of the facts of German opposition are concerned. For years the truth in this matter has been deliberately withheld or distorted. It can be shown that the intelligence services of the Western Allies had a fairly accurate picture of what was going on in Germany. This was the case even before Mr. Allen Welsh Dulles, as head of the continental branch of OSS, went to Switzerland (November, 1942) and established permanent contacts with the Underground. Nor is there any doubt that leading statesmen and diplomats in England and the United States also knew in detail about the structure of the German opposition movement and its aims, about its extent from right to left, about the participation of churchmen, about the obstacles and opportunities involved.

One can, of course, understand that all this information was treated as a top secret while the war seemed in the balance and Hitler's power still unshaken. It is less easy to defend—to say the least—that, on the evening of July 20, the Office of War Information in an official broadcast repeated Hitler's lie about the very small "clique" of ambitious officers—or, rather, outdid it. Moreover, this line of propaganda continued long after the end of hostilities, and still lingers on. The evidence which has come to light is still being belittled by writers and reviewers who like to depict the conspiracy as a sort of exclusive social gathering (*Herrenklub*) of hopelessly out-of-date gentlemen. One may acknowledge, however, that even this represents a certain progress when compared with the stage of complete silence. For quite a while the topic of the German opposition was taboo.[21] Early in 1945, an American correspondent in Europe

[20] Recorded by Mr. Morgenthau in the *New York Post* (November 24, 1947).

[21] The following facts are given on good American authority.

was forbidden, on direction "from highest Washington levels," to give out "any news about any specific resistance" to Hitler. Later on, when another correspondent traveled in Germany, one of the main sources of information, Fabian von Schlabrendorff's book *Offiziere gegen Hitler* (which had been published in Switzerland in 1946 and is now available in an abridged American translation)[22] was taken from him. Germans obviously were not supposed to read such a dangerous book.

This policy of censorship may have changed more recently; at least, in some places a different line seems to have been adopted. Thus a number of articles and pamphlets on the conspiracy were published in Germany during 1947.[23] But as late as the summer of 1946, when a former concentration-camp inmate and high civil-service officer in Darmstadt wrote an article on the Twentieth of July, in which he stressed the participation of the German working class in the plot, Headquarters in Frankfurt stepped in with a categoric veto. The same happened simultaneously when the Frankfurt radio station planned a commemorative broadcast. All other stations within the American zone were likewise forbidden to mention the "putsch." It is commonly said in Germany—and any such assumption is at least of symptomatic significance—that in the eyes of some Allied military personnel it is better to be an outright Nazi than a survivor of the Twentieth of July, for "they tried to cheat us out of our victory."

Fortunately enough, an observer in this country no longer requires either unusual boldness or any specific inside information to lift the veil or to eliminate the distortions. The basis for a correct appraisal, at least of the more dramatic events, has already been largely laid down. And it is to the credit of former American intelligence officers that they did not keep silent about what they knew, but decided to

[22] See p. 10, n. 1. Wherever possible, this study uses the American version, though it is marred by arbitrary changes and omissions.
[23] One article on the "History of the 20th of July" was even printed in *Neue Auslese* (August, 1947), a sort of Reader's Digest for Germany, edited by the Allied Information Service. The article is of some interest, though thoroughly tendentious.

open the way to truth. The first to break the story was Mr. Alexander B. Maley, a former lieutenant commander in Naval Intelligence. He wrote an article in February, 1946, "The Epic of the German Underground."[24] Then followed Mr. Franklin L. Ford, a former lieutenant in the Army with a special assignment to OSS, who in July, 1946, published an interesting essay on "The Twentieth of July in the History of the German Resistance."[25] And recently, more comprehensive information has been given out by Mr. Allen W. Dulles in his book, *Germany's Underground*.[26] In addition, printed information of various kinds has greatly increased. It can be supplemented with unpublished material, American and German alike. Not all of this is available for direct quotation now, and other definite gaps remain, which may never be filled. But in view of the developments of the last year, it seems a safe guess to assume that whatever appears in the future, whether taken from the files of the Gestapo or from papers and diaries which may still be hidden or buried under debris, whether based on Allied interrogation or neutral observation, is likely to underscore rather than minimize the scope of the opposition. The benefit of the doubt lies with, rather than against, the German Resistance.

[24] *Human Events*, Feb. 27, 1946. Another article followed (by E. A. Bayne, likewise a former intelligence officer), dealing with the Resistance in the German Foreign Office (April 3, 1946).

[25] *American Historical Review*, LI (July, 1946), 609-26.

[26] Published in April, 1947.

CONDITIONS AND POTENTIALITIES

1

German "Submissiveness"

THIS study is concerned with problems of opposition to a totalitarian regime (problems bearing not exclusively upon one people) and with historic facts relating thereto. The juristic or political aspects of "collective guilt" are outside its scope. Nor is there any intention to analyze the collapse of democratic Germany or to explain in detail the rise of the Nazis to power. In these fateful events, it would appear, very individual circumstances of the German scene worked together with very general circumstances; with the effects of Versailles as well as those of inflation and depression, with a spiritual impoverishment and a cultural crisis for which the Swiss author Max Picard has coined the suggestive formula of "Hitler in our selves." [1] This is not meant as an exculpation. The rogues and the careerists who joined the bandwagon cannot be excused on any ground, nor can cowardice or mass hysteria as such. And the supporting upper-class groups which fell for a fascist ideology, just as Mr. James W. Gerard and so many people abroad did, deserve no pity because of the rude awakening that lay ahead of them. In fact, few people had an insight into the true character of the Nazi ascendancy, and even today too many think of it in terms of an ordinary nineteenth-century revolution. They are likely, therefore, to apply to the oppositional movements the same nineteenth-century standards of class structure or party affiliation, and to overlook their broader meaning as a resistance of the human against the subhuman. What triumphed in 1933 was to a great extent the sinister forces which lie at the bottom of every modern society. They were swept to victory, as has been aptly said, [2] by a surprising "flank attack," largely carried by déclassés. They drew their broader support from the unemployed and a dispossessed lower

[1] *Hitler in Our Selves*, (Hinsdale, Ill., 1947).
[2] See Kurt Riezler, "On the Psychology of the Modern Revolution," *Social Research*, September, 1943, pp. 320-24.

middle class, a social "no-man's land." But once the rule of an energetic and fanatic minority was established, conditions were bound to change considerably.

Though nobody who knows totalitarian techniques will take the nearly hundred per cent pro-Hitler plebiscites of the years after the "national rebirth" at their face value, there is not the slightest doubt about the efficiency of the diabolic mixture of terror and propaganda which was characteristic of the Nazi system. It was not only fear, the "leadpipe" over one's head or the *blockwart* behind one's back, which caused the rush into the party or its affiliated organizations. It was, to some extent, the necessity of maintaining one's livelihood, but it was also an emotional urge and a pseudoidealistic appeal; this, in particular, seduced many young people. Moreover, a deceptive social amelioration was no less a psychological prop than would be, in subsequent years, Hitler's success in foreign policy. It is no basic excuse to say that foreign admirers of Hitler and foreign appeasers contributed largely to these psychological effects, though those in opposition always felt such an attitude to be truly a "stab in the back." Even such a man as Winston Churchill spoke of Hitler, in 1935, with admiration "for the courage, the perseverance, and the vital force which enabled him to challenge, defy, conciliate, or overcome all the authorities or resistances which barred his path." And Churchill echoed this praise as late as November, 1938.[3] But the aspect of international approval of Hitler's regime does not concern us in this discussion. What matters is, that large numbers of Germans enthusiastically hailed, or obligingly adhered to, a regime about the criminal features of which there could be no doubt. And even those

[3] *Great Contemporaries*, p. 265. See Dulles, *op. cit.*, p. 16. The case of foreign "coresponsibility" is aptly dealt with by Pechel (*op. cit.*, pp. 261-68), and in *They Fought Hitler First*. Churchill's initial admiration had repercussions as late as 1938, when he publicly stated: "I have always said that if Great Britain were defeated I hoped we should find a Hitler to lead us back to our rightful position among the nations." He added, however, "I am sorry . . . that he has not been mellowed by the great success that has attended him" (London *Times*, November 7, 1938, p. 12, col. 2). The quotation by Röpke and Jaspers (*Schuldfrage*, p. 70) is incomplete and overstates the case.

24

who paid only lip service were often forced into a system of concessions and smaller or bigger lies which could but have an emasculating effect.

It is a much-debated question whether or not this moral landslide can be referred to basic weaknesses in the German mind and an arrest in political development; or can be characterized as the natural outcome of pernicious trends in German history, either in its entirety or at least in its course since Luther, or Frederick II, or Bismarck. This question has been answered in the affirmative by an avalanche of books and pamphlets. Not all of them are of the propagandist type or mere Vansittartism. But whoever throws the stone in a self-righteous mood of moral superiority should carefully consult his own conscience or try to find an adequate testing ground. It is easy and may often be pharisaic to pass judgment without having been exposed to anything like the German experience after 1933, or without realizing that one might have likewise failed, perhaps, in smaller matters, as miserably as many Germans did.

Of a different character is the attention which recent German writers have given to the problem of how a highly cultivated people could submit to a criminal regime.[4] They have scrutinized certain critical aspects of German political, social, and spiritual traditions. "The real problem," as a Jesuit father put it, "is not Hitler, but the capacity to be infected by Hitler." Or, in the words of Karl Jaspers, the philosopher: "We must try to understand the germ of the evil which was planted long ago." This self-examination compares favorably, of course, with the attitude of those who suddenly discovered that they had never been Nazis; it has its undeniable and intrinsic merits. To sweep one's own doorstep seems a necessary part of any thorough house cleaning. Or, as the Catholic poet Reinhold Schneider set it down in stirring words: "Once the name of a family or a

[4] See as examples: Karl Jaspers, *Die Schuldfrage* (Zürich, 1946); Friedrich Meinecke, *Die deutsche Katastrophe* (Wiesbaden, 1946); Julius Ebbinghaus, *Zu Deutschlands Schicksalswende* (Frankfurt, 1946); Gerd Tellenbach, *Die deutsche Not als Schuld und Schicksal* (1947); Ernst Friedländer, *Von der inneren Not* (Hamburg, 1947).

25

people is incriminated, every single member is called upon to strive for a new and purer dignity."[5] Such a probing and such a call, however, clearly lead beyond political or juristic "guilt" into the metaphysical and religious sphere. And it may be noted in advance, that this was precisely the attitude which important figures of the German Resistance adopted. Long before defeat was imminent, they followed an aroused conscience; they took upon themselves the responsibility for crimes committed in Germany's name, and tried to atone for them by action or sacrifice. This was awareness of "sin" in a much deeper sense than that of a "faulty" historical development.

Moreover, if one admits that an infirmity in the traditions and in the moral fiber of German society, as well as a lack in individual habits of initiative or civil self-respect, made easier the acceptance of tyrannical power, there still remains the danger of undue generalization. In fact, the problem of German submissiveness has been obscured by a good deal of "begging the question." No appraisal can be fair which leaves out the factor of brute force, whether it was just threat of force or actual beating and torturing. Hundreds of thousands submitted to this rather than to any "attractiveness" or any material benefits afforded by the regime. If one takes the constant threat of the rubber truncheon into account, and then registers the weaknesses which are assumed to be typically German, there may indeed be more ground for marveling at the *limits*, than at the *extent*, of "submissiveness." As a matter of fact, it seems safe to say that resistance was much broader and more principled than current views of the German character or an insight into totalitarian dynamics could ever have suggested. And one may even add, that the German opposition to Hitler, by the very adversity of the conditions under which it had to operate, as well as by the response it made to this challenge in basically human terms, won a potential significance which transcends that of any merely national or social movement of liberation.

[5] Reinhold Schneider, *Das Unzerstörbare* (Freiburg i. Br., 1945).

26

Degrees of "Nonconformity"

Of course, no reliable estimate can be given of the relative strength of the four main groups among the German people: actual Nazis, nominal Nazis, non-Nazis and anti-Nazis. One group shades into the other. After screening more than one million cases of applicants for employment in the U. S. Zone, the American Military Government found that in 50 per cent of these cases there was "no evidence of Nazi activity."[6] Exactly what such negative findings mean may be debatable. But even allowing for a good deal of successful camouflage (and in this technique the Germans went through a thorough training during the Hitler regime), the percentage of approved non-Nazis remains amazingly high. In further critical evaluation of this figure, we may assume that it shades imperceptibly into that of nominal Nazis; and in addition, one remembers the complaint of Schlabrendorff who saw in the non-Nazis among the generals the greatest obstacle to action. "Their lack of backbone caused us more trouble than the wanton brutality of the Nazis." In fact, the problem of such an amorphous group is of a very complex nature. The same phenomenon exists in all totalitarian states, in the Soviet Union no less than in any other, and would deserve closer investigation. In Germany it certainly included those features of ostrich behavior which make neutrality despicable, but it included also the very broad element of what may be called *silent opposition*. In view of a claim to engulf all aspects of life—a claim more comprehensive in Germany than anywhere else as shown in Dr. Ley's boasting statement,"There is not such a thing as a private individual in National Socialist Germany[7]—it was already opposition of a sort; in fact, it was *potential resistance*, to show "no evidence of Nazi activity."

[6] H. Zink, *American Military Government in Germany* (New York, 1947), p. 142. On the subject of the questionnaires and their evaluation, see also M. Knappen, *And Call it Peace* (Chicago, 1947), pp. 124-28.

[7] For Dr. Ley's statement, see E. K. Bramstedt, *Dictatorship and Political Police: The Technique of Control by Fear* (London, 1945), p. 178.

Such an attitude implied some definite danger, though one mitigated by inconspicuousness. Hence silent opposition was easier for anonymous men and women to maintain than for prominent ones. But its importance should not be slighted. It indicates a reservoir of forces upon which active resistance might count, once power was wrested from an oppressive regime. At any rate, this "reserve front" suggests that broad sections of the people proved "water repellent" in a way; they continued to live a life of common decency; while making the barest minimum of concessions, they remained morally untouched; they never accepted the regime and never gave up hope, though they knew that they could not rise against the Gestapo with their bare hands.

This phenomenon, though difficult to describe in definite terms, can be amply borne out by observation. In factories and offices, talk changed automatically as soon as party members or informers were out of sight. There was among non-Nazis a silent, almost mysterious understanding. It became vocal, however, in biting jokes which spread like wildfire.[8] When the authorities on one occasion thought it wise to open a safety valve by permitting one uncensored edition of a Munich newspaper to appear at carnival time, they must have been shocked by what it turned out to be and by the rapidity of its circulation all over Germany.

Another striking feature was the spread of *Vereinsmeierei*, the increase in the number of small circles which discussed philosophical or religious, artistic or international matters. Even this form of "separatism" proved at times dangerous and might one day be answered by the dreaded ring of the bell at five o'clock in the morning. In fact, the non-Nazis shaded as much into the anti-Nazis as into the nominal Nazis. When Count Moltke, on the occasion of Mussolini's visit to Berlin in 1936, refused to have his office on Unter den Linden decorated and persuaded the other tenants also to refuse, this

[8] A collection of such jokes was published by J. A. Meier (*Geflüstertes. Die Hitlerei im Volksmund*, Heidelberg, 1946). The editor states that he was supported from all quarters in his collection of "butterflies."

was certainly more than showing "no evidence of Nazi activities."[9]

No less does the group of nominal Nazis defy generalization. In the minds of those who "went along," egotistic and idealistic motives were often inextricably interwoven. It can be argued that there was no more dangerous fallacy than the belief that by taking part in the regime or by joining the party, one would be able to mitigate excesses or "prevent things from becoming worse." In the over-all picture this was a fallacy, and often no more than a means of comfortable self-deception. Many observers hold the view that without the co-operation and competence of civil servants, managers, and other trained personnel, the Nazi administration and economy would have broken down in an early stage. And, in particular, the technocrats and "experts," with their abstract love for efficiency, duly come in for a large share of blame.[10]

But upon closer examination, other features also appear. It was not only that some high-ranking collaborators maintained a degree of independence and, sooner or later, began to sabotage the regime.[11] A few were or became outright opponents and worked effectively within the covering folds of the Nazi apparatus, even in Gestapo or SS disguise.[12] But besides these dramatic cases, open to more or less

[9] *A German of the Resistance*, p. 13.

[10] Riezler, *op. cit.*, pp. 328-29. See also Meinecke's chapter on "Homo sapiens and homo faber" (*op. cit.*, pp. 50-63).

[11] The outstanding example of this type is, of course, Hjalmar Schacht, who since 1936, at the latest, co-operated with the conspirators and, according to one witness (Mrs. Strünk) was urged by them to remain in office. Another is Albert Speer, who, in the last phase, sabotaged the "scorched-earth" policy. He has been given comparatively high praise by Mr. Trevor-Roper, who otherwise has so little to say about the genuine opposition.

[12] Along with the renegade Count Helldorff, the Berlin chief of police, the main examples are Art. Nebe, chief of the Reich Criminal Office and SS General, who fell as a victim of the Twentieth of July, and Hans Bernard Gisevius, a survivor of the plot and witness at Nuremberg, whose memoirs (*To the Bitter End*) and whose work for OSS in Switzerland have gained him reputation. Both men undoubtedly rendered most valuable services to the Underground, and played a risky game with courage and skill. But neither got rid of the Gestapo atmosphere, and Gisevius' book should be read with critical reservations. At the start he asserts that, "It was the custom for newly appointed

serious objection, there is another very important, though elusive phenomenon. In the technical branches of the civil service the number of non-party members remained comparatively large, and here even nominal Nazis often succeeded in maintaining "out-of-date" professional ethics.[13] Not a few who survived persecution and terror owe their lives to this fact, or found sympathy and help in most unexpected quarters. There is no doubt that within the co-ordinated services, whole groups were in silent but effective opposition, opening whatever loopholes they could. The United States Strategic Bombing Survey, in supplementing its earlier summary reports in 1947, had this to say of "German morale":[14] "Quietly working within the confines of the machine, there were elements opposing National Socialism. As far as the police were concerned, it is clear that the detective force contained substantial numbers of the old supporters of the Republic, who had mainly belonged to the Social Democratic party. Such men might go so far as to arrange escapes for intended victims of the Gestapo by entering their names in the missing-persons files, after having warned them of an impending arrest. It was known to 'insiders' that there were quite active cells of this nature in government agencies, such as the Ministry of the Interior, the Ministry of Justice, the Ministry of Labor, and certain courts and prosecutors' offices, not to mention local government services. Such persons could, and sometimes did, effectively sabotage Nazi law enforcement."

assessors to begin their careers as assistants to the political police" (p. 37). This one falsehood alone should be sufficient to warn the reader. Gisevius obviously knew less than he pretends to know; and there were important facts which he did not know at all. He has some axes to grind and not a few things to explain for himself; in many parts of the book, the truth is impaired by his obvious resentment at being kept at arm's length by the conspirators.

[13] For the Ministry of Labor see: J. Eckert, *Schuldig oder Entlastet* (Rewi, 1947), pp. 196-207.

[14] *The Effects of Strategic Bombing on German Morale* (Washington, 1947), p. 96.

Attitude Towards Jews

Within this silent work of opposition and sabotage, the German attitude toward persecuted Jews needs special consideration. That anti-Semitism (often cloaked either as anticapitalism or anticommunism) had a broad appeal and gave occasion to scandalous profiteering goes without saying.[15] But that it met with more or less general approval or connivance is simply not true. When, after the outbreak of war, the British Government published "Papers concerning the Treatment of German Nationals in Germany,"[16] they included therein German letters which voiced a certainly widespread popular indignation at the so-called "spontaneous" pogroms of November, 1938.[17] And in the report of the British Consul General in Frankfurt (December 14, 1938), we read:[18] "It seems to me that mass sexual perversity may offer an explanation for this otherwise inexplicable outbreak. I am persuaded that, if the Government of Germany depended on the suffrage of the people, those in power and responsible for these outrages would be swept away by a storm of indignation if not put up against a wall and shot."

The British observer may have been too optimistic; and the German civil servant who wrote to another British official that "the German folk have had nothing whatever to do with these riots"[19] surely overstates the case. It is more to the point that an SS brigade leader had to admit in a letter to Himmler:[20] ". . . native anti-Semitic forces were *induced* to start pogroms against Jews during the first hours . . . though this inducement *proved to be very difficult*."

[15] On German anti-Semitism and its background, see the recent study by W. Gurian, *Antisemitism in Modern Germany*, Conference of Jewish Relations (New York, 1946), pp. 218-65.

[16] *Germany No. 2* (1939). This British *White Book* was concerned with anti-Jewish atrocities only.

[17] *Ibid.*, pp. 6-7, 18-19.

[18] *Ibid.*, p. 20.

[19] *Ibid.*, p. 18.

[20] *Nazi Conspiracy and Aggression*, I, 137-38 (Italics are the author's).

Besides these negative evidences there are, however, many instances of sympathy, help and positive support which can be established on firm ground. Definite groups, such as the Quakers, and Protestant as well as Catholic societies, were engaged in very extensive relief work. Of course, few were the voices of those who protested publicly, and they were soon silenced. Among the men who dared to speak up unmistakably, the Dean of St. Hedwig, Monsignor Bernhard Lichtenberg, may be mentioned.[21] Since the pogroms of November, 1938, he would pray himself, and have the congregation of the Berlin cathedral pray, for "Jews and persons in concentration camps." These and other demonstrations (including a protest against the "mercy killing" of the insane) led to his arrest in October, 1942. While in prison, he offered to transfer to the ghetto of Lodz; he died on his way to Dachau in November, 1943. Protestant parallels are not lacking.[22] And there were many individual acts of which, of course, no record has been kept: acts of concealing Jews, of helping them out of the country, or providing them with food tickets. Some evidence has come to light in the trial against the so-called *Solf-Kreis*, and this whole sphere of a principled anti-Nazism cannot simply be passed over. The name of Otto C. Kiep stands for a group in the Foreign Office which participated in such activities. Nor should a figure like Elisabeth von Thadden, headmistress of a private girls' school, who was close to Frau Solf, be left unmentioned.[23]

[21] See Alfons Erb, *Bernhard Lichtenberg* (Berlin, 1946), esp. pp. 42-47, 50-53, 61.

[22] To give only one example, reference may be made to the "atonement" service in the packed main church of Dahlem in November, 1938. For other examples, see H. Fraenkel, *The German People versus Hitler* (London, 1940), pp. 131-32.

[23] On the *Solf-Kreis*, see Arthur Nicolson in *Spectator* (1945, p. 456), Dulles, *op. cit.*, p. 88, and Pechel, *op. cit.*, pp. 88-93. Frau Solf, widow of the late German foreign minister and Ambassador to Tokyo, her daughter and sister, and her friends, were active in shielding Jews and in other humanitarian work of anti-Nazi character. Elisabeth v. Thadden had the misfortune of being successfully spied upon by the Gestapo. She was hanged after July 20, as were some of her friends, among them the former consul general in New York, Otto C. Kiep. Frau Solf, after a long trial, was saved, it is said, by intervention of the

She was not an active opponent in the political sense but her very being and example was a source of strength for others and a rebuke to the regime as long as she lived.

In addition, an insight into the more systematic and outright conspiratorial work of such humanitarian circles can be won from Ruth Andreas-Friedrich's *Berlin Underground*.[24] This report about the resistance group "Uncle Emil," though couched in fictional terms, has all the ring of truth. Whoever knows of these things will even recognize some of the pseudonyms. There was no political aim upon which all members of the circle would agree, save a passionate antinazism (resulting in a defeatist campaign), and above all a profoundly human urge. As can be seen time and again, the basic "potential" of opposition rested upon ethical and religious convictions, or the irrepressible demands of human decency. "What we do," writes Mrs. Andreas in her diary, "is individual work, done by thousands upon thousands of Germans, is done on behalf of humanity despite oppression, persecution and tyranny." And she adds very aptly: "Here is something that should not be forgotten when the day of reckoning comes, by those who have an easier time than we in being kind and helpful human beings."[25]

There must have been many such groups in other cities (examples are known from Munich and Augsburg), and in Berlin alone there must have been many more than one; otherwise the result actually achieved would be inconceivable. Mr. Weltlinger, a member of the Berlin City Council who is at present in charge of Jewish affairs, has

Japanese Ambassador. Several of her friends, however, were murdered shortly before the liberation, among them the Secret Councillor in the Foreign Office, Richard Kuenzer, and also Herbert v. Mumm, Count Albrecht Bernstorff, Dr. Kempner, and Dr. Zarden, both former Undersecretaries of State. About Kiep, see also Dorothy Thompson, in: K. O. Paetel, *Deutsche Innere Emigration* (New York, 1946), pp. 18-20. On Elisabeth v. Thadden, a memorial address is available, given by her sister, Frau Ehrengard Schramm-v. Thadden. A brother, also, was a leading lay member of the Confessing Church, imprisoned by the Nazis as well as by the Soviets.

[24] New York, 1947, with an introductory note by Joel Sayre.
[25] *Ibid.*, pp. 98-99.

recently stated,[26] that the majority of "Aryans" were never affected by Nazi anti-Semitism and that in Berlin five thousand Jews were hidden by their compatriots. A pitifully small number, to be sure, when compared with those who perished, but the number of Germans who risked their lives to bring this result about must have been anything but negligible.

4

Intellectuals and Churches

The discussion of silent opposition shading into open nonconformity or definite forms of underground work leads to the two groups which were specifically faced with the problem, or rather charged with the task, of keeping up human integrity and spiritual resistance: the intellectuals and the churches.

Against no other group has heavier blame been leveled than the professors and journalists, writers and artists. And if they represent, to some extent, the conscience of a nation, no standard, in fact, can be strict enough. Again, it has been argued, as in the case of the civil servants, that a widespread (or unanimous) protest of the German intellectuals would have damaged the regime beyond repair, or even brought it down before it was definitely entrenched. This may be so, although such an assumption seems more out of date—that is, in line with nineteenth-century conceptions of the "political professor," or of the role of a revolutionary "intelligentsia"—than were the actual plans and actions of the German resistance. At any rate, nothing occurred in 1933 in the way of spiritual upheaval, and examples of weakness and corruption were abundant. The invention of "German" mathematics and other forms of intellectual prostitution, as well as the numerous "somersaults" of scholars and writers, one can only recall with shame. It is also undoubtedly true that many trends in German academic life had paved the way for an excessive nationalism and an "anarchy of values" upon which the brutality of Nazi dic-

[26] *Die Neue Zeitung*, September 2, 1947.

34

tatorship and the shallowness of Rosenberg's "myth" could thrive. While in the universities the number of "old Nazis" was exceedingly small, and in almost any such case personal motives of frustration could easily be pointed out, co-ordination proceeded with disgusting speed and often anticipated actual enforcement.

All this has to be stated with the seriousness which such a phenomenon deserves. It falls under the heading of the *trahison des clercs*. And to counterbalance the one-sidedness of accusation, it is not sufficient (though it would be necessary for the sake of fairness) to name those who did not give in: some "grand old men" (and younger ones too) in philosophy and education, in history and jurisprudence, in Romance languages and philology, in economics and physics.[27] In part it may also be credited to the university professors that an average of 25 per cent of the students did not join the Nazi student association, though this abstention gravely endangered their enrollment as well as their professional careers. Moreover, other redeeming facts can be pointed out, which were presumably of broader influence: some periodicals retained their editorial standards, such as the *Hochland* and the *Weisse Blätter*, the *Corona* and the *Deutsche Rundschau;* also a considerable number of writers, poets, and artists can be named who refused to conform and "knuckle under," or were in open opposition.[28] It should not be assumed that all of this did serious harm to the regime, but it heartened those who resisted.

[27] Some indications in Ambassador Dodd's memoirs. For more detail, see Pechel, (*op. cit.*, pp. 105-6), and the testimony of a Swiss student about his impressions at the University of Munich during the war, and about the attitude of the students (*ibid.*, pp. 104-5). See also Röpke (*op. cit.*, pp. 82-84). As to the other side of the picture, see M. Weinreich, *Hitler's Professors* (New York, 1946).

[28] The poets Werner Bergengruen, Hans Carossa, Ricarda Huch, Reinhold Schneider, Wilhelm v. Scholz, Walter v. Molo, Rud. Alex. Schroeder, Fr. Georg Juenger, and Ernst Wiechert may be mentioned. For documentation see Paetel, *Deutsche Innere Emigration*. That others like Gerhart Hauptmann (whom upon his death the Soviet occupation authorities praised very highly) cut a sorry figure, is understood, to say nothing of the outright converts or fellow travelers. It may be mentioned that Ricarda Huch, who died in November, 1947, has prepared two volumes on "Figures of the German Resistance."

And a more striking phenomenon became apparent, once the torrential waters had run their course: the indestructibility and the regenerative force of the spirit, as proved under this very Nazi regime. Evidences of this can be seen in the intensity of intellectual life in small circles and neighborly associations, but also in the attitude of the reading public at large, and in theater programs and literary production in general. On April 18, 1942, the *Frankfurter Zeitung* discussed the phenomenon of a "certain reaction," that is, the preference of the readers for "old" books and "more profound works." We have learned of a bookseller in a small Württemberg town who made his shop the center of a lively exchange between patrons and authors;[29] in the shopwindows of publishing houses and bookstores Nazi writings, of course, were on display, but a thriving business was done along different lines, with less boring offerings made available, if necessary, "beneath the counter." Theological tracts and "classics," as well as translations from foreign literature, were in heavy demand; popular editions of the authors of antiquity, including the pre-Socratic philosophers (in two languages), of Chinese thinkers, of Dante, and Thomas Aquinas appeared.

Scholarly production also continued to a surprising degree, even in wartime. More often than not it proved free of any Nazi tinge. A recent reviewer in an article entitled "German Historiography during the War" (a very critical one, incidentally), finds that the "garden of traditional scholarship was rapidly shrinking" and that there were no open clashes.[30] But he also states that "the way in which certain

[29] See Wilh. Hoffmann, *Nach der Katastrophe* (Tübingen, 1946). Some of the following facts are taken from Röpke's chapter on intellectual resistance (*op. cit.*, pp. 87-104). See also W. W. Schütz, *Pens under the Swastika* (London, 1946), and the chapter "Bookstores" in his *German Home Front*, pp. 216-20.

[30] F. Gilbert, in the *American Historical Review*, October, 1947 (Quotation on p. 53). The reviewer's comment, however, is in this author's opinion, too pessimistic. A preliminary investigation of the co-ordinated *Historische Zeitschrift*, for example, shows that there was more undisturbed integrity than could be expected and "open clashes" (esp. in the reviews) were not lacking. Some additional, and very necessary corrections to Gilbert's partial appraisal have been made by W. Gurian in the same journal, January, 1948, pp. 437-38.

special questions were handled by the more traditionally inclined historians implied a rejection of the assumptions underlying . . . Nazi conceptions" and resulted "in a real addition to our historical knowledge." This seems an understatement rather than an overstatement. Rejection of Nazi tenets was, in fact, often quite explicit. At the meeting of German historians in 1943, for example, a leading medievalist stated, in clearly heterodoxical language, that the emergence of the "German" from the "Germanic" was due to the influence of antiquity and Christianity. As to scholarly research, medieval history in particular made rapid strides. And the garden did not shrink so much. In 1946, the University of Bonn issued a list of publications of the years 1939-45.[31] While obviously leaving out all Nazi books and other writings placed on the Allied "Index," the catalogue numbers about three thousand titles, mostly in the field of cultural sciences. Some, of course, suggest escapism, or at least a choice of subject matter out of the danger zone. But certain points of emphasis are very striking, as is the range of interests in general. In the first place, the scope is European, and for national culture, there is a definite "restorative" tendency, whether expressed in turning to biblical traditions, or to Plato and Aristotle, or to Meister Eckhart, Nikolaus von Cusa and Jakob Böhme, or to Humboldt and Schleiermacher, Goethe and Stifter. A former German professor now living in Switzerland (who generally is rather critical of his colleagues beyond the border), says very aptly,[32] that in the insistence on intellectual con-

[31] *Neuerscheinungen der deutschen wissenschaftlichen Literatur, 1939-1945*, Teil I (Bonn, 1946), 131 pp. Teil II, dealing with medicine and the natural sciences, was not available. According to Wilhelm Hoffmann (*German Books, A selective critical bibliography*, Chicago, 1948—, I, 5-6), Stuttgart librarians plan an exhibit of "German Literature during the resistance, 1933-1945" (*not* "resistance literature"), which promises to bear out the view of "the preservative and creative powers which existed in Germany."

[32] Röpke, *op. cit.*, p. 91. One may compare this verdict of a critic who kept contact with things German, with that of Thomas Mann or the summary and irresponsible statement of William L. Shirer, that the Inner Emigration "produced nothing of worth—a frightening phenomenon" (*End of a Berlin Diary*, p. 218).

tinuity and integrity, a definite sort of opposition can be seen. And he adds that there is every reason to pay respect to the civilian courage which was shown in many cases.

In fact, nonconformity again overlaps with more or less subtle forms of resistance. And from there, it is only one step to a campaign of deliberately undermining Nazi tenets or calling for opposition to a tyrannical regime and to totalitarianism in all its aspects. Even the ostensibly co-ordinated "bourgeois papers," such as the *Frankfurter Zeitung*, used certain means of attack—the "commercial page," for example. If no other way was available, they sanctimoniously reprinted some of the more stupid announcements of the party press: for example, the one about the Japanese as "yellow Aryans," or that about tomatoes as "northern" fruit of the South. Individuals could go further. In 1935 a former Rhodes scholar, Adam von Trott zu Solz, one of the outstanding figures within the active conspiracy, edited and commented on the writings of Heinrich von Kleist,[33] the German poet of the early nineteenth century, whose attacks on Napoleon's tyranny could easily be read into contemporary events. In the Introduction, the editor said unmistakably that Kleist became a rebel because he saw the dignity of man impaired, and that he set his hope upon the common sense of decency out of which the people would free themselves of the demoralizing effects of despotism. There was a good deal of such indirect shellfire on the part of German writers, whether they appraised Demosthenes as against Philip and Burckhardt as against Nietzsche, or discussed Cromwell or Robespierre, Pilsudski or the mass hysteria among sixteenth-century Anabaptists. The same technique of camouflage was successfully applied by the *Deutsche Rundschau* in articles meant for a broader public (and, in fact, circulated in mimeographed sheets). They dealt with subjects such as Siberia or the South American dictator Lopez, subjects the implications of which were not difficult to discover. More frankly, the same periodical stated in April,

[33] *Heinrich v. Kleist, Politische und Journalistische Schriften* (Potsdam, 1935). See: *Innere Emigration*, pp. 70-71.

1941: "Megalomania is one of the most dangerous diseases of a people."

One may ask how these indirect attacks could be carried out and independence preserved under the very eyes of the Gestapo and the Ministry of Propaganda. In one case (Ernst Juenger's *On the Marble Cliffs*),[34] it is said that Goebbels himself was delighted because the book seemed to single out the sinister figure of a "Chief Forester" (Göring). Moreover, Goebbels was intelligent enough to see the deadly dullness of the official literature and the party press; he gave to the theater at least a certain freedom. In writing and teaching, there were the loopholes mentioned before.[35]

But there were also definite limits. Rudolf Pechel, a member of the active conspiracy since the early days and the editor of the *Deutsche Rundschau*, was arrested in April, 1942, when one of his articles had the bad fortune of being sent from London back to Germany by the British Broadcasting Company.[36] He, his wife, and his friends were tried, and during three years of "interrogation" and concentration camps he narrowly escaped death. The fate of another writer of the opposition, Ernst Wiechert, has become well known in this country.[37] In an address to "The German Youth" which he gave at the University of Munich in 1935, he implored his audience "never to keep silence when the conscience commands to speak out," because nothing in the world "corrodes the marrow of a man and a people as does cowardice." He had eventually to pay in Buchenwald for his personal integrity. To other intellectuals and university teachers who joined the active resistance, reference will be made later on. Whatever the "sins" of the profession, a picture painted all in black seems hardly adequate. Nor was intellectual opposition an esoteric

[34] New York, 1948.

[35] Ritter (*op. cit.*, p. 249) speaks of the "services of the university officials of most of the German states, in upholding German learning."

[36] Pechel, *op. cit.*, pp. 294-303.

[37] See his own report in: *Der Totenwald: Ein Bericht* (Zürich, 1946); trans. as *The Forest of the Dead* (New York, 1947). His two important speeches (of 1935 and 1945) are published in *The Poet and His Time* (Hinsdale, Ill., 1948).

affair, understandable only to the initiate who lived in the past. It would be more appropriate to speak of a movement of "reaction," in the best sense of the word—that is, of a return to eternal sources, and of an emergence or revival of energies which placed political opposition on a broader and more fundamental basis.

This holds good for the churches more than for any other group of the opposition. Here again, to be sure, hesitation and compromise were not easy to overcome, nor was the basic antagonism clear from the beginning. It was only sectarians such as Quakers and Mennonites, or "*Ernste Bibelforscher*," who never wavered. They consistently practiced passive resistance, but were small in numbers.[38] As to the Catholic Church, the Vatican, by concluding a concordat, at first tried to secure some external barriers against totalitarian claims and the spread of New Heathenism. In fact, the highest authority in the church started the series of international treaties which contributed to the legitimacy and respectability of the Nazi regime. Protestantism, on the other hand, was hampered in its resistance by the tradition of a positive relationship between church and state (*Landeskirchentum*) and by certain features of its social structure. Moreover the Lutheran branch of Protestantism prevailing in Germany stemmed from a doctrinal position which placed emphasis on the spiritual rather than on the outside world, on the salvation of souls rather than on the Christianization of society. In fact, to Luther the external order of things, an order perverted by sin, was of subordinate significance. It could not be "reformed" by human effort, but only through faith and Christian love. Thus in Luther's view (different from that of Calvin) the Kingdom of God was purely transcendental. These traditions and attitudes spelled conservatism, politically and socially; they were opposed to direct action and stressed the biblical injunction to "render unto Caesar the things that are Caesar's."

[38] For the *Bibelforscher* in the concentration camps, see: Kogon, *op. cit.*, pp. 41, 269-71. Members of "free churches" numbered less than 1 per cent of the German population (about 600,000 in 1933, as compared with the 41 million members of the established churches). Cf. Carl Mayer, "The Crisis of German Protestantism," *Social Research*, November, 1943, p. 400.

But the National Socialist attack upon both churches, as well as upon Christianity in general, soon brought the latent conflict into the open. This part of the story has so often been recorded,[39] that a few remarks will be sufficient here. Besides the trumped-up charges against individual Catholic priests and Catholic orders, besides the invasion of the Protestant churches and the church administration —an invasion carried out by the pro-Nazi "German Christians"— there arose the fundamental incompatibility of principles symbolized in Cross and Swastika. Thus it was not only the Gestapo interference or the attempt to conquer the churches from within, against which the Catholic bishops and the Confessing Church raised their voices. It was the Nazi system in its basic features: totalitarianism, with its complete disregard of the sanctity of individual life and its flouting of the most elementary notions of justice; the racial reinterpretation of the Christian faith; the deification of Hitler and the glorification of the "blood community of the chosen German people."

There was no way of dodging this issue, once it had become clear, and anyone who reads Cardinal Faulhaber's sermons on the Old Testament, or the pastoral letters of the German bishops, or the official pronouncements of the Confessing Church, will no longer be inclined to assume that "meek submission" was the rule. As early as 1935 a manifesto against "racial mysticism" was read from Protestant pulpits, whereupon seven hundred pastors were arrested. In a memorandum, moreover, which the leaders of the Confessing Church addressed to Hitler at Whitsuntide, 1936, they stated:[40] "When blood, race, nationality, and honor are regarded as eternal values, the first commandment obliges the Christian to refuse this valuation. When the Aryan is glorified, the Word of God teaches that all men are sinful. If the Christian is forced by the Anti-semitism of the Nazi Wel-

[39] See the books by N. Micklem, *National Socialism and Christianity* (Oxford, 1939), and *National Socialism and the Roman Catholic Church* (Oxford, 1938), also A. S. Duncan-Jones, *The Struggle for Religious Freedom in Germany* (London, 1938), Michael Powers, *Religion in the Third Reich* (New York, 1939), Hugh Martin and others, *Christian Counter-Attack* (New York, 1944).

[40] H. Martin, *op. cit.*, p. 35. For the manifesto of 1935, *ibid.*, p. 34.

tanschauung to hate the Jews, he is, on the contrary, bidden by the Christian commandments to love his neighbour." With the same turning to fundamental human questions, a Pastoral Letter of the German bishops stated in 1942: "We wish particularly to stress that we are not only standing up for religious and ecclesiastical rights, but also for the ordinary rights of mankind . . . without them the whole of Western culture must collapse."[41]

This was no mere sermonizing. It was lived and corroborated by those hundreds of pastors and churchmen who were removed from their pulpits and offices or sent to prisons and concentration camps. According to American sources "some eight hundred Catholic priests and between three and four hundred Protestant ministers" perished in Dachau.[42] While among the Catholic priests probably non-Germans prevailed, the Protestant ministers are, in the main, likely to have been Germans.

But within this general and broadly accepted picture of spiritual resistance, some critical aspects need discussion. First, how far did church opposition extend? There were differences in tactics within the Catholic fold and differences, specifically, between the so-called "undestroyed" Protestant churches in southern and western Germany (Hannover), which were less endangered, and the old Prussian church (Union) which found itself actually with its back against the wall. Nowhere in the Protestant camp was there unanimity. Even in Berlin (with its suburb Dahlem containing the unofficial headquarters of the Confessing Church), there were, in 1937, only 160 ministers who belonged to the Confessing Church; 40 were German Christians and 200 "middle-of-the-roaders."[43] These figures seem to have some bearing upon the problems of opposition in general. In a way, National Socialism can be regarded as an extreme consequence of nineteenth-century secularism. Hence it followed that "liberal" Protestantism,

[41] *Ibid.*, p. 30. See complete text in the *New York Times*, Sunday, June 7, 1942.

[42] Knappen, *op. cit.*, p. 95. According to a recently published list, 2,600 ecclesiastics passed through Dachau, the majority being Polish and German.

[43] C. Mayer, *op. cit.*, p. 426 n.

42

which was permeated with an idealistic philosophy of culture and the "metaphysics of progress" (Tillich), had more belief in *laisser-aller* and less power of resistance to the Nazi regime. The "radicals," it must be understood, were the "conservatives"; that is, those who adhered to an undiluted doctrinal position and a thoroughly pessimistic estimate of the "natural," the "demonic" forces in the world. While this movement was undoubtedly led by the orthodox part of the clergy and cannot be held representative of the church membership to an equal degree, theological interest among laymen also spread to an amazing extent.

But then the other question arises, whether this was not again some sort of escapism, or whether the insistence on a primarily spiritual opposition was not fatally delaying political opposition. Dr. Niemöller, the best known among the leaders of the Confessing Church, has frankly admitted the justice of this reproach, at least to the extent that the Protestant Church awoke to the danger only when it was attacked in its own and innermost concerns. When Protestant representatives of Germany met with those of western European countries and the United States in Stuttgart (autumn, 1945), they acknowledged responsibility for not having resisted the Nazis earlier and more effectively. They felt that the church shared the "guilt for the war" because no attempt had been made to overthrow the government in time.[44]

This statement, like any other example of critical self-examination, stands on its own merits, and should not be mistaken for a matter of expediency. A "holier than thou" attitude would have contradicted the very impulses which came to light in the church opposition. But whether these impulses could have or should have led to jumping into immediate political action, is quite a different proposition. It seems to have been in the nature of things that spiritual protest and the defense of the Gospel came first. Only so was there reached a unity born of suffering for the sake of the Christian faith. Only so could passive resistance develop, though slowly, into a frontal attack

[44] On the Stuttgart declaration, see Knappen, *l. c.*, pp. 119-20.

upon the very essence of National Socialism and into a "total" opposition against any worldly totalitarianism. From a historical point of view it may well be asked whether the churches, by taking a stand within their own confines, did not provide the forces of active resistance with a harder core and a sharper cutting edge than any external "revolt" could have done.[45]

This leads to a last question, which concerns the effects of the church opposition. It certainly forced the government to recoil more than once from extreme measures. We know that the gauleiter of East Prussia, for example, warned the party against driving the peasant population (German and Masurian Protestants) into open rebellion. The experiment of the *Reichsbischof* Müller failed miserably. And in 1936 a truly "popular revolt" in Münsterland succeeded in restoring the crucifix to school buildings.[46] There were other retreats, while at the same time persecution increased, until, with the outbreak of war, the "cold" method of removing and killing off ministers by deliberately sending them into the front line was widely applied.[47] Yet, too drastic clashes had to be avoided. Thus, action was withheld, for example, in the case of the Bishop of Münster, Count von Galen, when he preached his famous "three sermons" in 1941, or when in 1942 he openly attacked the criminal practices of the regime in the occupied territories.

More important perhaps was the effect upon the churches themselves. They gained unmistakably in prestige and vitality. And

[45] Gisevius' remark (*op. cit.*, p. 216) that with Niemöller's arrest in the middle of 1937 "the last chance for a real popular opposition movement" or "any sort of civilian revolt" disappeared, seems to be one of the apodictic statements of which he is so fond. In addition, this remark is contradicted by the whole tenor of his book, by his constant insistence upon the indispensability of boring from within and planning from above.

[46] A. S. Duncan-Jones, *op. cit.*, pp. 217-19. In 1938, in spite of official obstruction, the number of Catholic pilgrims to St. Annaberg reached the record figure of 130,000. They chanted defiantly: Our Führer is Christ. (H. Fraenkel, *op. cit.*, pp. 160-61).

[47] Up to April, 1942, 7,000 members of the Protestant clergy had been called up and 698 had been killed (H. Martin, *op. cit.*, p. 42).

44

though doctrinal questions were taken more seriously than in preceding decades, the boundaries between the confessions greatly decreased in importance at the same time. Liturgical movements worked toward the *Una Sancta*, and a common front appeared. As Von Preysing, the Archbishop of Berlin, declared in 1937: "... never before ... have we been so deeply linked in love and sympathy with our brothers who differ from us in creed."[48] This Christian solidarity was an essential feature of the German Resistance. It expressed itself in many cases of mutual support or combined action. Moreover, for the first time since the middle of the nineteenth century, lost ground was reconquered by religion. Not only were Christian and communist prisoners often drawn together in mutual esteem, as Pechel and Wiechert saw; it also appears that the courage displayed by ministers and churchmen won them associates from among Marxist elements which had long been alienated from Christianity. This is amply borne out by the co-operation within the leading groups of the conspiracy, and by the Christian socialism of the Kreisau circle.[49] It is true that the masses which, for example, packed the Protestant services in Dahlem (though their attendance was spied upon) did so, not from religious motives only, but also to express opposition in the only form available to them. Yet they could not fail to be caught by the intense spirit displayed in the churches. Sometimes, after a manifesto was read or when the Gestapo went into action, the congregations began spontaneously to sing Luther's hymn, "A mighty fortress is our God." Thus it became a song of political defiance and of religious confession at the same time.

But another aspect of the church struggle must also be stressed. Beginning from a merely religious point of view, opposition turned against any form of oppressive regime, whether the attack upon the dignity of man was of national socialist or any other color. Totali-

[48] See the chapter on "Christian Solidarity" in Duncan-Jones, esp. p. 254.
[49] See also: P. van Husen, "The 20th of July and the German Catholics," *Dublin Review, July, 1946, p. 3.* The book by F. Muckermann, *Der deutsche Weg; aus der Widerstandsbewegung der deutschen Katholiken*, was not available.

tarianism (like peace) was "indivisible," and red concentration camps were no better than brown or black ones. This attitude created difficulties when Americans after the war took up contact with German churchmen. Was their anti-Sovietism not a reflection of Goebbels' propaganda, or a relic of nationalist and reactionary trends, or a clumsy speculation upon disunity among the then allies?[50] It may be assumed that a better understanding of the issue and the inner necessity of this attitude has taken place in the meantime. At any rate, it should be clearly noted that genuine church opposition was possible only on a basis of principles which were kept free from opportunism, and therefore maintained the same antitotalitarian front after the fall of the Nazis. "If we claim to be Christians," Pastor Bonhoeffer once said, "there is no room for expediency."[51] Only on such a ground could an uncompromising attitude be preached and the protest of the churches grow into underground work and active political resistance. It was not easy for the Confessing Church to maintain a clandestine organization for the training of ministers, an organization which had to use all the ruses of political conspirators. Such practices might very well press upon a sensitive conscience. It was even more difficult for twentieth-century Christians to fall back, as it were, upon the theories which Calvinists and Jesuits had taught some three centuries before, and which laid it upon the "pious" to overthrow or even dispose of "Godless" authorities. Not that the conflict was necessarily seen in such a historical perspective, but the reference may illustrate the weight which a struggle over a profound moral issue, once overcome, was likely to add to the political front of opposition.

It is to this front that we have now to turn.

[50] Even in so fair-minded an interpretation as that of M. Knappen (*op. cit.*, Chaps. XI and XII), such repercussions can be seen.

[51] *Contemporary Review*, CLXVIII (1945), 208.

PLANS AND ACTIONS

1

Early Nuclei

THERE would be little point in trying to state at what precise time active political opposition to Hitler started in Germany. In some of its early aspects it was a mere continuation of the struggles preceding the Nazi accession to power and also, in part, of the defense of the Weimar Republic. It was leftist and antifascist, though changing its character in accordance with the conditions of "illegality." The first to be outlawed were the Communists; deprived, with one stroke, of almost all their leaders, but trained in conspiratorial techniques, they went underground and created the pattern for the organization of oppositional cells. A summary of the rules which were drawn up for these cells has been preserved.[1] The basic requirement was that "members must, under no circumstances, be aware of the activities of any cell but their own." Besides extensive measures of self-protection, emphasis was placed upon sabotage in factories and upon propaganda. There is no doubt about the large amount of subversive work that was done in these fields, and about the supreme courage displayed by many individuals.

The other more or less liberal parties—Socialist, Centrist and Democratic—indulged for some time in the illusion of legal political opposition. There still seemed hope for a restoration of the rule of law and of parliamentary control. In fact, did not the elections of March, 1933, prove that in spite of terror and intimidation, the non-Nazi parties still held a majority? While the Communists felt sure that Hitler was working for their own ends, merely by accelerating the doom of bourgeois society, other leftist parties were more likely to think in terms of a temporary setback. As the chairman of the Social Democratic party declared at the party's last mass meeting in Berlin: "Strict masters do not rule for a long time."[2] But these

---

[1] H. Fraenkel, *op. cit.*, pp. 70-71.

[2] Evelyn Lend, *The Underground Struggle in Germany* (New York, 1938), p. 17.

illusions were destroyed, bit by bit; by the Reichstag fire and the persecutions following in its wake, by the tricky "Enabling Act" of March 23, which practically disposed of parliament as well as of the Reichspresident, by the dissolution and expropriation of the trade unions, and finally by the outlawing of all parties except the Nazis in July, 1933. Nothing but illegality was left.

It has often been asked why force was not countered by force from the very beginning, or why resort was not had to a general strike, which had proved so successful in defeating the Kapp putsch thirteen years before. Those who ask these questions are apt to overlook the bewildering and paralyzing effect of entirely new experiences and the weight of evolutionary and legalistic traditions to which Social Democrats as well as trade unions clung. Moreover, the Nazi coup d'état was no putsch; it was carried out in pseudolegal and pseudo-democratic form, as a "gradual revolution"; it had its own popular support, particularly among the unemployed and the lower middle classes. And even leaving this split in the masses out of account, there was no unity within the German proletariat. Communists and Nazis, though fighting their frequent street brawls, had joined hands more than once: in August, 1931, in support of a referendum against the Social Democratic government of Prussia, as well as one year later, in support of the wildcat strike of the transport workers in Berlin. And they would do so again, on directive from Moscow, during the interlude of Soviet-Nazi liaison from August, 1939, to June, 1941. There was then, as one must realize, a potential totalitarian front crossing the proletarian front, and there was little inclination, on the democratic side, to swap a Russian for a German dictatorship. These facts played a considerable part in the history of the German resistance. Socialists and Communists kept moving along different lines. Not even in the phase of "popular front" policy (1936-38)[3] did a real fusion occur. And when at the last moment, in June, 1944, some of the Socialist conspirators approached

[3] See the Berlin appeal of the "Deutsche Volksfront" of 1936 in *Deutsche Innere Emigration*, pp. 41-42.

a clandestine Communist Committee, the result was fatal because of Gestapo infiltration into this central cell.[4]

From the very start, however, there were younger men in the radical camp, as elsewhere, who tried to break away from the pre-Hitlerian party lines and party concepts. In the summer of 1933, a pamphlet was written in Germany (and later published abroad) under the title: *New Beginning—A Secret German Manifesto*.[5] It not only insisted upon unity within the proletarian front and co-operation with liberal-democratic forces, but set out to interpret more realistically the nature of the Nazi dictatorship and to draw practical conclusions therefrom. Instead of arousing a mass movement, too costly in human lives, emphasis was to be placed upon building up "a strong and firm organization composed of experienced functionaries, well trained theoretically as well as practically, with contacts in the important workshops and possibly in other sections of society." While in a long-range view, this program, which looked ahead to a great international crisis, proved sound, the "illegals" meanwhile went through bitter experiences. The "New Beginners" themselves were driven into exile; Socialist and Communist committees also had to establish themselves abroad, and Democratic and Centrist leaders likewise were sooner or later forced to leave the country. They all

[4] See Dulles, *op. cit.*, pp. 73-74. About German Communist tactics and the orders received from Moscow, see *ibid.*, pp. 98-100. If the "SS Report on the 20th of July" (see Note 2) can be trusted, the man most successful in infiltration work was Heinrich Müller (Gestapo Müller). Before 1933 he had been a member of the Bavarian political police. He is credited with planting the V-men (liaison men) in Communist and Socialist cells. It seems plausible that the phase of Soviet-Nazi liaison made this task considerably easier. This does not mean that all Communists followed Moscow's orders. Individuals certainly carried on in their own way, and the new phase made no difference for Communists in concentration camps anyway. There was hardly the "complete standstill" in Communist underground work, of which Mr. Dulles speaks (*ibid.*, p. 99). About revived Communist activities after June, 1941, see the declaration of the "Rhineland Conference" (Dec., 1942) in *Innere Emigration*, pp. 45-47. See also Pechel about the "Gruppe Saefkow" (*op. cit.*, pp. 93-95).
[5] Abstracts and comments in E. Lend, *op. cit.*, pp. 28-30; *Innere Emigration*, pp. 39-41; J. B. Jansen and St. Weyl, *The Silent War*, pp. 129-32.

kept contact with their party remnants, but co-operation between the three main groups was hampered by mutual distrust. And there was grave disappointment because of the lack of support from the outside world.

In spite of these setbacks, the pace of activity soared for a while. The country was flooded with illegal pamphlets and leaflets. They were smuggled in by "border secretariats" or printed in clandestine workshops. All sorts of clever devices were used to camouflage the propaganda campaign and to make distribution anonymous. Pages could be filled with the description of these practices or with quotations from underground literature.[6] Reports were also smuggled out of Germany which passed on intelligence—political, economic, military—or told about instances of opposition, about slow-down campaigns in workshops or the rejection of Nazi candidates in factory elections.[7] And the political committees in exile were eager to disseminate encouraging information from inside Germany.

But the Gestapo closed in with increasing efficiency and the working population had to bear the brunt of the counterattack. Losses were very heavy. In 1934 the *Manchester Guardian* wrote of the "ten thousand unknown heroes."[8] In 1935 a new wave of terror set in. People with competence in underground party work seemed to agree that in view of existing conditions there was rather too much than too little going on. They were critical of the great numbers who, as the Austrian Socialist Otto Bauer wrote, were "attracted by the romance of clandestine activity and the adventurous appeal of the fight with the police." Could mass propaganda seriously threaten the Nazi regime, or did the stealing and hiding of some weapons alter

[6] Details can be found in Fraenkel, *op. cit.*, pp. 89-114; Lend, *op. cit.*, pp. 30-50 (covering the years 1933-37); Jansen-Weyl, *op. cit.*, pp. 78-108. Also in W. W. Schütz, *German Home Front* (London, 1943); in the *Inside Nazi Germany* reports (London, 1939-40); the *Inside Germany Reports* (New York, 1939-44); and other more sporadic publications.

[7] See Dulles, *op. cit.*, p. 103, about the "Green Reports" and their usefulness to the "foreign offices of many governments."

[8] For this and the following, see Jansen-Weyl, *op. cit.*, pp. 78-81.

the situation to any degree worth the sacrifices involved? Was the moral effect of placards posted or slogans painted on the walls in proportion to the risks taken? Instead of merely annoying the Gestapo by methods which proved suicidal, it seemed more important to save the cadres of resistance within the labor movement and the trade unions, socialist as well as Christian; to keep old nuclei intact, to select and train new collaborators carefully. One should not lose sight of the long-range effects of this reorientation and of the "reserve front" of silent opposition which could be counted upon. But the change in tactics meant that since 1935 a certain diminution in the scope of traceable antifascist activities occurred.[9]

Not enough material is available for a broader discussion of the part which the alleged *Röhm-putsch* and the purge of June 30, 1934, played in this connection. It was certainly wishful thinking on the part of the early "illegals" to believe that this was the beginning of the end.[10] The sequence of events was to disappoint them severely; it seems obvious today that the clash took place primarily within the Nazi ranks, and only secondarily between the SA and the army, with the SS reaping the benefits. Indirectly, however, the "night of the long knives" has a definite bearing upon the history of active resistance. It was not known at that time that the number of victims amounted to 1,076; *only* 77 murders were officially admitted. Yet the brutal savagery of the ruling clique opened the eyes of many, and the extent of the purge suggests that some anti-Nazi planning was involved in the crisis.

The side issue of an attack upon the regime had been heralded by a strikingly worded address which Vice Chancellor Von Papen delivered to students at Marburg on June 17, 1934. The speech had been written by the Munich lawyer, Edgar J. Jung, who belonged to a group of "neoconservatives," composed of determined Protestants and Catholics alike. They, like many other elements of the Right, had

[9] See in Jansen-Weyl the chapters on "Organization for the Future" and on "A Formula for Survival" see also Lend, *op. cit.*, pp. 51-56.

[10] See evidences of this belief in Lend, *op. cit.*, p. 38.

long ago broken with the nationalist and materialist views of Hugenberg's[11] pseudo conservatism, but they were also aware of the dangers implied in certain pseudoliberal extremes; that is, in an atomized and de-Christianized society, in a secularistic mass civilization which lent itself to demagoguery and dictatorship. Most of them stood for federalist principles, for a European order based on national autonomy (rather than on centralized sovereign states) and on corporative organization patterned after the trade unions. Jung himself, who had observed the rise and character of the Nazi movement in Munich at close quarters, voiced his warnings in a book with the provocative title: *The Rule of the Inferiors* (*Die Herrschaft der Minderwertigen*). He was hardly under any illusions regarding the reliability of Von Papen, but he had accepted a position under him as a point of leverage. Pechel, who belonged to the same circle, asserts that Jung and his friends had definite plans for overthrowing the government and that the Marburg speech was meant as a signal for action.[12] However this may be, connections certainly existed with Treviranus, who had led an anti-Hugenberg and anti-Nazi front of the moderate Right in the early thirties, and with Dr. Brüning, the Centrist leader and last democratic chancellor to defend the Weimar Republic. It seems that an active part was assigned to both these men in the planning; both escaped the purge by a hair's breadth only. How substantial the connections were with Klausener (the head of Papen's ministerial bureau and of the "Catholic Action") and with Von Bose (another of Papen's aides), or with the generals Von Schleicher and Von Bredow cannot be ascertained. But it seems likely that their assassination was more than a mere settling of old accounts. They all, like Jung and scores of other opponents of Nazism, fell as victims on June 30.

Whatever the inside story of this episode, it confirms the view that the German opposition shifted its ground and changed in character. It grew beyond and across party lines and was carried by groups

[11] The leader of the Nationalist party, and Minister of Economy in Hitler's first cabinet.
[12] Pechel, *op. cit.*, p. 77.

which banded together rather spontaneously and out of common motives of political and moral indignation.[13] Here appears the basic phenomenon which was previously called the rise of "the human against the subhuman." There had been instances of this kind from the very beginning. Von Schlabrendorff tells[14] how, early in 1933, he and some of his conservative friends liberated Ernst Niekisch, a radical socialist writer, who with other anti-Nazis was kept in an SA cellar. Niekisch in turn gave shelter, during the purge of June 30, to one of Schlabrendorff's intimates, Ewald von Kleist, a scion of an old Prussian family. Niekisch had become known as the manager of a publishing house and editor of a widely read periodical, both with the name *Resistance* (*Widerstand*), a title which did not yet have a specific anti-Nazi tinge. Later on, however, he wrote a clandestine pamphlet with the title: *Hitler, a German Disaster*. That he found himself co-operating with the young conservative opposition is already a prelude of things to come. He carried on his fight until arrested for high treason and imprisoned for life in 1937.

There were many other groups of men and women, loosely organized around local or personal points of crystallization. One (the Roemer circle) agreed early upon the necessity of Hitler's assassination. Through liaison people in the Berlin *Kommandantur* and the Foreign Office, they received regular information about the Führer's schedule, but the plans never came off.[15] Idealists like Von Halem were involved in these attempts. In addition, some individuals and outsiders followed their solitary paths. It appears certain by now[16] that it was such a "solitary fanatic," a communist carpenter named G. Elser, who planted the bomb in the Munich beer cellar. It exploded

[13] Something of this motivating force is grasped intuitively in Carl Zuckmayer's play: *Des Teufels General* (Stockholm, 1946). He has an engineer who is head of the plotters' group in the air ministry say: "One day I felt ashamed about being a German. Since that time I cannot find rest until the thing is over" (p. 162).

[14] *Op. cit.*, pp. 10-11.

[15] Details in Pechel, *op. cit.*, pp. 81-84.

[16] See Gisevius, *op. cit.*, pp. 393-411.

on November 8, 1939, just five minutes after Hitler "providentially" had left the speaker's platform. While Himmler demanded the arrest of forty "Bavarian legitimists" as accomplices, and the blame was later laid upon the British Secret Service, the public largely believed that the attempt was manipulated by an *agent provocateur*. But Elser seems to have acted entirely on his own. And it can be assumed that there were more bomb explosions than is publicly known. Mr. Shirer, who certainly did not pay any sympathetic attention to symptoms of resistance around him, mentions two in one Sunday night alone.[17]

But it seems more pertinent to our study to stress the fact that within the early groups of political opposition many of those names appear which point ahead to the history of the Twentieth of July, and that their membership clearly illustrates the spread of a deeply rooted spirit of opposition through all classes—a spirit which derived directly from fundamentally new experiences under the Nazi regime. Thus, seeds were planted in these years by individuals and groups, not with a view to immediate action but in preparation for action. Pechel, who had many-sided contacts, lists among other well-known figures: the Communists Saefkow, Jacob, and Bästlein; the Socialists Ernst von Harnack (the son of the famous theologian), Dr. Mischler, and Markwitz; the Centrists Andreas Hermes and Jakob Kaiser. He pays special tribute to the men who were to lead the *Rote Kapelle*—the resistance group located mainly in the Air Ministry, but spreading beyond it—Schulze-Boysen and Arvid Harnack. He also lists industrialists such as Von Halem and Reusch or the men in Stuttgart around Robert Bosch (who financed the *Deutsche Rundschau*), and in addition he names artists and professors, lawyers and doctors and individuals from all walks of life.[18] Of interest also is an observation which Schlabrendorff made in 1938.[19] Having been engaged for

[17] William L. Shirer, *Berlin Diary* (New York, 1942), p. 218 (Sept. 20, 1939).

[18] See the chapter: "Resistance of Individual Groups, 1932-1944," *op. cit.*, pp. 71-113.

[19] *Offiziere gegen Hitler*, p. 21. The passage has been left out in the American version.

54

some time in conspiratorial work on a local and provincial scale, he found upon his return to Berlin that the character of the opposition had changed; while previously it had been composed of elements which played a leading role in pre-Hitlerian political life, it consisted now, not of a firm organization but of a number of co-operating and overlapping circles. It suggests itself that they were tied together by common ethical convictions, rather than by social affiliations. Into this picture seems to fit the founding of the German Liberty party (*Deutsche Freiheitspartei*) in 1937–38. Its first leaflet stressed "the dignity of the human personality" as a rallying cry for all anti-Nazis, and it insisted that the political aim could not be a mere return to Weimar.[20] This was a line upon which many would agree.[21]

The question must then be asked, whether there were other more solid nuclei besides the underground cells in the working population or the leftist parties, and besides the more recently formed, looser groups of people who were aroused in conscience. In particular, did such active nuclei exist in such as yet unpenetrated key positions in the state as the Foreign Office, administration, and army? To this question, no affirmative answer can be given for the early years. As to the Foreign Office, it is true that many individuals shared in oppositional work (Von Twardowski, Von Etzdorf, Aschmann, aside from those who are to be given specific mention). Some passed on intelligence, as for example, Hitler's interpreter, Dr. Paul Schmidt.[22] Like other civil servants, they resented the corruption and arbitrariness (if nothing else) with which they had to cope in fulfilling their duties. They felt loyalty to the nation rather than to a particular government. It is also true that Bernhard von Bülow, Secretary of State in the early years, warded off successfully Nazi infiltration into the central office, and held concessions to a minimum. In fact, Nazi

[20] *Innere Emigration*, pp. 43-45.

[21] Thus H. Fraenkel (*op. cit.*, pp. 206-9 and 240-52) discusses the Liberty party (and its short-wave operations) as an expression of conservative opposition as well as of a leftist one.

[22] For more detail, see the article by E. A. Bayne (p. 22, n. 24). About Schmidt, see Dulles, *op. cit.*, p. 44.

55

foreign policy had to find its own agency outside, in the Bureau Ribbentrop. When the latter was organized in April, 1934, first with a special mandate for "Disarmament Questions," but soon expanding into general affairs, the Foreign Office placed Dr. Erich Kordt as a liaison officer in the rival body. In assuming his position, Kordt was instructed by Von Bülow not to correct Ribbentrop's errors, but to leave him enough rope to hang himself. This seems characteristic of an official "wait and see" policy in the first years, a policy which still indulged in certain illusions. The eventual result, however, was the formation of an important cell of resistance under Ribbentrop's very eyes. It may be mentioned that Kordt also provided for a link with Dr. Brüning, and that Von Kessel, an associate of Kiep, was made liaison man to the War Ministry.[23]

As to the administration, no definite front was formed, though again outstanding individuals are known who voiced and practiced opposition in an early stage. There was, for example, the case of the State Secretary in the Prussian Ministry of Interior, Herbert von Bismarck, who protested against the lawlessness of persecution.[24] Failing in his attempt to win over other non-Nazi ministers, he resigned. Another case was that of Landrat Theodor Steltzer, whose name will recur in connection with the Kreisau circle. In 1933 he circulated a memorandum in which he severely condemned the regime in most of its aspects, while stressing the religious basis of opposition.[25] He was arrested in 1934 on the charge of high treason, but released with-

[23] Only these few hints can be given here, with some more data in the next section. Dr. Kordt is expected to give his own report (and an inside story of Nazi foreign policy) in a book which he is now preparing for publication. Obviously he belonged also to the group "Uncle Emil"; he appears in R. Andreas-Friedrich's book under the pseudonym "Erich Tuch." When Ribbentrop took over the Foreign Office in February, 1938, Kordt became chief of his ministerial bureau. The book by Dr. Kordt, *Wahn und Wirklichkeit; die Aussenpolitik des Dritten Reiches* (Stuttgart, 1947), has been received during the proofreading. It deals with the resistance movement and the author's personal part in it in a very reserved way only. Cf. pp. 113–14, 124–28.

[24] Schlabrendorff, *op. cit.*, p. 12.

[25] An abstract of this memorandum was available. See also Dulles, *op. cit.*, p. 90.

out trial. It will be shown that Goerdeler, price commissar from 1934 to 1935 was undoubtedly working through all these years for close contacts between anti-Nazis inside as well as outside Germany, and for coalescing active opposition among his acquaintances in the government and in private business.[26] In 1937 he went to England and the United States. It seems that about 1936 even the "mercurial" Schacht, against whose financial policy of backing the rearmament program Goerdeler had fought in vain, began to come around. We have been given a dramatic (and probably overdramatized) story of a secret meeting between Schacht and a commanding general, which was planned by Gisevius early in 1937.[27] In late 1936, according to another source of information, Schacht sent a confidant to Chief of Staff Colonel General Beck, and asked him whether he was prepared to take action against Hitler. Beck is said to have answered that to change the regime was a civilian affair, but if the civilian opposition took the initiative, the army would not fail them.[28]

It was indeed a civilian affair, and so it should continue to be. By 1937, however, all oppositional circles agreed upon one experience. There was under the Nazi system not the slightest chance for the success of an unarmed movement—neither for a revolution in barricade style, for a popular uprising and other forms of spontaneous resistance, nor for a revolution from above, to be carried by conspirators inside the fold or by top figures in society and bureaucracy. Whatever the importance of the early nuclei, it was imperative to break the coercive power of the Gestapo and the SS. And this could be done only by the "bearers of arms." People began to speak of the "generals," a term which had not been in use in Germany before.

[26] Besides sources to be cited later, some material is contained in a memorandum of Frau Goerdeler (written in March, 1946). See also Franklin L. Ford, *op. cit.*, p. 615.

[27] Gisevius, *op. cit.*, pp. 205-10.

[28] In a somewhat different vein Halder, the successor to Beck, is said to have retorted to Schacht in 1938: "the people who put Hitler into power should get rid of him . . . . you elected Hitler . . . . We soldiers had no right to vote" (Dulles, *op. cit.*, p. 44).

This brings up a number of questions which need special consideration.

2

Crisis of 1938

Before discussing certain problems involved in army resistance and then returning to the basically civilian aspect of opposition, something should be said about the first combined plan of action, which has received comparatively little publicity. It crystallized with the approaching Czechoslovakian crisis in the summer of 1938. The Chief of Staff, Colonel General Beck, who had already opposed Hitler's Austrian adventure in March, was by now convinced that the Führer would plunge the world into war. At a secret staff meeting he declared that he would not stand for such a catastrophic policy. Later on he is said to have received promises from every army group commander that no one would accept an appointment as his successor. Beck also circulated a memorandum proving Germany was incapable of winning a European war. His opinion was shared at that time by Commander in Chief von Brauchitsch, who took the memorandum to Hitler and added a warning of his own.[29]

But this was not to remain a matter of merely professional criticism or military obstruction. Beck and his advisers in the Intelligence Services held the view that once the sinister perspective was shown to the German people the spell would vanish which Hitler's previous successes in foreign policy (rearmament-Rhineland-Austria) had cast upon so many. If the Nazi regime could be denounced as clearly warmongering, an overthrow would be easy. The conspiratorial groups which had drawn more closely together since 1937 agreed upon these conclusions. They decided to forestall a Euro-

[29] See Ford, *op. cit.*, p. 616; Dulles, *op. cit.*, pp. 41-49. The chronological sequence up to Beck's dismissal is not quite clear and the underlying presentation by Gisevius is particularly confused and confusing. The main facts, however, are confirmed by other sources.

pean war, and regarded the threat to peace as an ideal occasion to secure broad popular support for a revolt against the regime.

There is no doubt that this analysis of public opinion was correct. Anyone knows that who had an opportunity to observe the German people during the crisis which preceded the Munich accord. Not only was Chamberlain, as the bringer of "peace in our time," hailed hardly less enthusiastically by a misinformed German public than by the English; other striking things also happened. When Hitler made the theatrical gesture of having one of the new armored divisions march through Berlin, the demonstration was received with icy silence. So was Hitler himself when he appeared at the balcony of the Reich Chancellery on September 27.[30] At the height of the international tension there were obvious symptoms of a severe psychological crisis for the regime.

In anticipation of this, plans had been laid by the military to capture Hitler and to put him on trial. The commanders of the Berlin district (Von Witzleben) and of the Potsdam garrison (Von Brockdorff) were in the plot. In addition the chief of the Berlin police (Count Helldorff) was won over, and an armored division under General Hoeppner took up position in Thuringia to intercept the Munich SS in case they tried to relieve Berlin. It can hardly be said that the plans were deficient from a technical point of view, or that not enough striking power was provided to carry the putsch through.[31]

[30] Eye-witness reports in R. Andreas-Friedrich, *op. cit.*, p. 213, and Constantin Silens, *Irrweg und Umkehr* (Basel, 1946), p. 184. See also Gisevius, *op. cit.*, p. 324; Kordt, *op. cit.*, pp. 122–23, 131–32.

[31] Ford, who knows only of the division in Thuringia, seems to criticize the adequateness of the plan rather unjustly. The full extent of the preparations is borne out not only by Gisevius and Halder (who testified publicly), but also by personal information which Beck gave to Pechel in the house of Colonel General v. Hammerstein (Pechel, *op. cit.*, p. 151). Issue must also be taken with Mr. C. L. Sulzberger's statements (*New York Times*, March 18, 1946). In a very sketchy article ("Full Story of Anti-Hitler Plot"), he assumes that it was only in 1942, after the removal of Witzleben, that his "ambitions drove him into anti-Nazi channels." He makes a similar statement about Hoeppner. Though the search for "frustrated" ambitions is a very popular device, it simply does not cover the case of men who were in the plot as early as 1938.

The weak point, rather, was the underlying assumption that the Western democracies would oppose Hitler's designs on Czechoslovakia, thereby making apparent the threat of a general war.

It can be shown that Goerdeler was informed about the military plans and tried to pave the way for them.[32] In 1937 and again in the summer of 1938 he went to London to warn his British friends and to advocate a strong line against Hitler. In this the oppositional group of the Wilhelmstrasse concurred. And thus one of the strangest incidents in the history of any Resistance came about.[33]

After several secret messages had already been conveyed to Chamberlain and Halifax, and after consultation with Beck, the Secretary of State in the German Foreign Office, Baron Ernst von Weizsäcker (who had succeeded Bülow) arranged for a rather unusual step. Through Erich Kordt, information and secret instructions were sent to his brother, Theodor, who at that time was Chargé d'Affaires in London. Having asked to be received in utmost secrecy, Theodor Kordt was invited to come to the backdoor of No. 10 Downing Street during the night of September 5. In his conversation with Lord Halifax he emphasized the necessity for the British government to take an unqualified stand against Hitler's plan to use force. In case such a firm stand was adopted by the statesmen of the Western powers, the German army would refuse to fight against Czechoslovakia. This, at least by implication, meant a promise to overthrow the Hitler

[32] Gisevius admits that Beck was in contact with Goerdeler, but states that Halder was not. In a sentence which may be quoted as highly characteristic, Gisevius writes: "We had not let Goerdeler into our secret. That was really not very kind of us" (*op. cit.*, p. 327). Throughout, he tries to give the impression of a merely military coup d'état, with himself, of course, and possibly Schacht as civilian instigators. He mentions neither Goerdeler's parallel steps nor the participation of Weizsäcker and the Foreign Office. Instead he more or less clearly pretends that the action in London was his. ("We [!] went even farther and informed the British government" *ibid.*, p. 319.) Dulles, unfortunately, follows Gisevius here (as in other places) rather too closely.

[33] The incident is briefly mentioned by Dulles (*op. cit.*, p. 42), and by Ford only in a footnote (*op. cit.*, p. 616). As to source material, see Ford, *ibid.*, p. 612, n. 5. More detail is now available, some in the article by Bayne (see p. 22, n. 24); the main source, however, has not been published.

regime. The same communication was made to an influential conservative member of the House of Commons, Sir Horace Wilson, and, as will be shown later, it reached Winston Churchill too.

While awaiting British action, Beck was prepared to press the button. A setback, of course, occurred when Chamberlain decided to fly to Berchtesgaden. But in the critical days at Godesberg, with Hitler increasing his demands, and during the ensuing deadlock, there still seemed to be reason for hope. Beck, however, had meanwhile been dismissed, and the plan of making his resignation the signal did not come off. But his successor, General Halder, was prepared to go ahead, and orders were about to be issued for the action to take place on the morning of the twenty-ninth. All was ready, as the Foreign Office was informed by the War Ministry. But then, at midday on September 28, word came that Chamberlain and Daladier had accepted the invitation for a conference at Munich. This sensational news ran like an electric shock through government circles, and the whole scheme collapsed.

Two weeks later Goerdeler wrote to an American friend: ". . . the German people did not want war; the army was ready to do everything to prevent it. . . . the world had been warned and informed in time. If these warnings had been heeded, and if one had acted accordingly, Germany would be free of her dictator today and could turn against Mussolini. In a few weeks we could begin to shape a lasting peace which would be based on justice, reason and decency. Germany with a government of decent men would have been prepared to solve the Spanish problem together with France and England, to remove Mussolini and to create peace in the Far East in cooperation with the United States. The way might have been open for good cooperation in the economic and social fields and for pacification between labor, capital and the state, for an elevation of moral concepts, and for a new effort to raise the general standard of living. . . . "[34]

[34] The full text of the letter of October 11, 1938, is printed in German in: Goerdeler, *Politisches Testament: Dokumente des anderen Deutschlands*, herausg. v.

One may find this interpretation overoptimistic in its confidence and its sweeping character. Of course nobody can say whether the putsch would have succeeded. Beyond any doubt, however, is the broad element of promise in it, and its more than military perspective. The action was planned not only in order to prevent a war which Germany was bound to lose in the end. It was thought of also in terms of European pacification and the restoration of human decency in international as well as in domestic matters. That gives to this episode its historic place in the stream of tragic events. And whoever assumes the attitude of a judge should not permit himself to pass too readily over the night of September 5, 1938. With the marked sense of fairness which the Indians had found characteristic of the "tall Christian," Lord Halifax said to Theodor Kordt a few days after Munich: "We were not able to be as frank with you as you were with us. At the time that you gave us your message we were already considering sending Chamberlain to Germany." The same fairness should be applied to the evaluation of a crisis during which German generals and civilians, for the sake of a higher duty, cast aside conventional standards and acted in a way which certainly does not bear out "submissiveness" to an abstract idea of the state or to an inherited code of blind obedience.

It is not necessary to follow this up by mentioning the subsequent military efforts to forestall war in 1939 and to be prepared for a coup. They are less important because Halder did not possess the caliber of Beck. And they did not have the same broad implications, though again they were accompanied by civilian actions—for example, the visits of Schlabrendorff, Goerdeler, and Pechel to London and the new warnings transmitted to the British Foreign Office through Erich Kordt—or by the labors of Von Trott and Von Hassell. Part of this

---

Friedrich Krause (New York, 1945), pp. 57-64. The quotation is taken from parts of the letter, as given in Dulles, *op. cit.*, pp. 47-48. Elsewhere in the original letter Goerdeler said that whatever the external successes of the regime, he knew that "the dictators are nothing but criminals" and that "Hitlerism is poison to the German soul."

story has been narrated by Mr. Dulles mainly on the basis of Halder's testimony at Nuremberg. There is no point in repeating it here.[35]

We have instead to turn from the one important incident, to a broader discussion of the part which the military sector played under the Nazi regime and in the whole of the resistance.

3

Military Sector

The relationship between army and party implies one of the major problems in the history of the Third Reich. It cannot be covered by any easy formula, neither by that of an allegedly "natural" clash of two "elites"—an older one, aristocratic and somewhat degenerate, versus a younger one, plebeian and biologically superior (the Goebbels explanation)—nor by the contrary assumption, likewise generalizing, of an allegedly "natural" alliance between "Prussian militarism and Nazism" (the official American thesis during the war). In reality the problem has run through several stages, and defies simplification. For one thing, it shaped up differently for the various branches of the armed forces. The German navy, founded in the days of William II, had always been more nationalistic and less "Prussian." Its historic nucleus was negligible as far as it went back before 1870; since its modern beginnings, it had been recruited from all of Germany and its officers' corps was predominantly middle-class. This holds good even to a greater degree for the air force, a recent creation without traditional roots and particularly attractive to the technically minded. As far as any general verdict is possible at all, navy and air force showed little resistance; they were more nazified than the army. Only one admiral stands out in the ranks of the military conspirators —Canaris, a very unconventional figure, serving as head of the In-

---

[35] See Dulles, *op. cit.*, pp. 49-52; also Gisevius, *op. cit.*, pp. 327-76. Much information about this phase is given in the Von Hassell *Diaries* (New York, 1947), pp. 5-72 (particularly about his contacts with Sir Neville Henderson). See also Schlabrendorff's talk with Winston Churchill (*op. cit.*, pp. 21-22).

telligence Division of the War Ministry. And the plotters in Göring's Air Ministry were outsiders. Moreover, it was the army, naturally, which assembled the largest numbers in wartime and was, in peacetime, the only organized power able to deal with the Gestapo and the SS. In this respect, the situation was very different from that which gave importance to the navy revolts at Kronstadt and Kiel in 1917 and 1918 respectively.

Hence, it is to the army and its background of Prussianism and aristocratic concepts that our attention must turn. As far as this military sector of the Third Reich is concerned, there can be no doubt that a certain cleavage existed from the beginning. Whatever the contribution of the Munich *Reichswehr* to the rise of the party, or that made by commanding officers in East Prussia (Von Blomberg, and Von Reichenau) to Hitler's seizure of power, it was a support given with the same reservations which other upper-class groups maintained, inside as well as outside Germany. The hope was indulged of being able to use the "drummer," the "Bohemian corporal," the man with the funny mustache, as a tool, and then to throw him away. This was a *proton pseudos* of large and fateful consequence. But besides the compromising attitude of military opportunists, there was that of uncompromising foes. The outstanding figure among these opponents is the Chief of Staff in the first year, Colonel General von Hammerstein-Equord—the "Red General," as he was often called—a passionate anti-Nazi and a man of deeply religious convictions. In January, 1933, he urged a military action against Hitler, but was prevented by Hindenburg, on the ground that politics were not the army's business.[36]

The line of aloofness became then, in fact, the dominant one during the early years. It seemed to be in accordance with Prussian military traditions and with an aristocratic code, though the principle of keeping out of politics had had very different meanings before 1914, when meddling with public affairs seemed improper, and after 1919, when the *Reichswehr* was a sort of state within a state. With the

[36] Dulles, *op. cit.*, p. 26.

64

conditions prevailing under the Nazi regime, however, this "hands-off" attitude was bound to gain a completely new meaning; it amounted practically to toleration of crime and murder on the part of those who had power to avert them; it thereby contradicted another, most honorable militarist and aristocratic tradition, that of *noblesse oblige* and of the protection of the weak. It is true many officers felt shame and indignation not only at the murder of Von Schleicher and the way it was hushed up, or at the incredible intrigues to which their own Commander in Chief, Von Fritsch, fell a victim; not only at the racial legislation which hit quite a number of their comrades or comrades' families, and destroyed the ties with, and the very existence of, so many Jewish veterans of the last war.[37] They felt the same about the brutal things which took place outside their professional circle, about the scandals and outrages which they could not help seeing in the streets or hearing about. And the Protestant churches were never more crowded with officers in uniform—a rather unusual sight. There is no doubt that the army gave strong support to the Confessing Church and saw in the attack on Christianity a basic threat. A book published under the auspices of the War Ministry stressed this point. The whole climate of the regime, its boasting, its demagoguery, its appeal to the basest instincts, was certainly as anti-Prussian as possible. And yet no immediate reaction followed from the cleavage.

Of course, one can understand why Von Fritsch did not raise the

[37] There were some cases of protection afforded to Jewish ex-officers by the *Reichswehr*. But the army looked on when the wreath which Jewish veterans had placed on the tomb of the unknown soldier was removed and the veterans' associations were forced to expel their Jewish members. As to the "Nuremberg laws," the army remained exempt for a while, because full application would have involved many prominent officers, particularly among the landed gentry. But the procedure of the authorities became gradually stricter, and there was the case of the Jewish widow of General Hoffmann (a notable leader in World War I), who, after being subjected to shocking indignities, committed suicide in 1938 (Fraenkel, *op. cit.*, p. 204). In general, the wave of arrests in November, 1938, was specifically directed against Jewish ex-servicemen. In individual cases, high officers made some efforts to intervene, but with little success.

standard of revolt for his own defense; but there were enough general issues of honor and morality which would have furnished a starting point, and the War Ministry was amply supplied with evidences of Nazi crimes.[38] But none of these opportunities was seized upon, and discipline was too strict to allow spontaneous military actions against murder, plunder, and arson when they raged through German cities in November, 1938. It was only at the last minute, during the Polish campaign, that a genuine militarist tradition reasserted itself. Examples are known of regimental commanders, who, with armed interference, put a stop to the looting and the killing of civilians by the SS, and real battles were fought between soldiers and the black squadrons. But these instances of professional ethics and decency were not backed up or followed through, and another opportunity of saving the honor of the German army was missed.[39]

While this sin of ommission must be stated unmistakably, it is obvious that army aloofness was a sort of opposition in the same sense as the term has been applied to other "water-repellent" parts of the population. Even more effectively so. In fact, the army was the only social body within the state which was able and seemed determined to close all loopholes of infiltration. Party membership ceased under the colors, there were to be no politics, and the repeated "offers" of Dr. Ley to organize the soldier's leisure time ("strength

[38] According to Gisevius, this was one of his and Nebe's main activities in the early years (e.g., pp. 144, 162, 171). His connections were with the *Abwehr* (Intelligence Service). Hammerstein, significantly enough, is not mentioned at all in Gisevius' book, except in a recapitulating remark (pp. 430-31).

[39] Based on personal information. According to Von Hassell's diaries (p. 84), even Von Reichenau, who began to waver, "risked a word of protest against the SS bestialities in Poland," and Blaskowitz, commander of an army in Poland and later of the army of occupation, "wanted to prosecute 2 SS leaders (one of them the notorious Sepp Dietrich) for looting and murder. But in vain" (*ibid.*, pp. 79, 100). *The New York Times* also reported (Jan. 30, 1940) that Blaskowitz "took exception to the methods employed" (p. 9, cols. 3-5). See also Schlabrendorff, *Offiziere gegen Hitler*, p. 35 (the passage is omitted in the American version). Another occasion arose in June, 1941, before the attack on Russia, when Hitler formally abolished the rules of warfare (see p. 70, n. 45).

66

through joy") were successfully warded off. Moreover, it was well known that Nazi functionaries, when called up, had a hard time in the army, and that top sergeants found an especial pleasure in deflating them. As an emigré author quite correctly puts it:[40] "The Reichswehr never even tried to conceal the opinion that young men joining straight from Nazi schools must first be purged of most of the ideological rubbish they had been taught . . . " and in the military academies there was no "new-fangled nonsense" of any sort. Nor was the premilitary training of the Hitler Youth looked upon any more favorably. As an old officer sarcastically remarked: the constant marching results in disgust for anything military and—in flat feet only. Some cases are also reported to the effect that preference was shown to recruits who had been members of Socialist youth organizations. "That's the type of man we want."

As a result, the army in the early years was to a large extent Nazi-proof. And this probably increased the illusory feeling that one could wait for some fruits of Hitler's revisionist and rearmament policies without incurring the danger of being carried away. The army actually appeared as a refuge for potential resisters. When Von Hammerstein was told about the growing number of high-school graduates who intended to choose a military career, he is said to have answered: "I know, this is simply another form of inner emigration."

In truth, however, the integrity of the army was gradually whittled down, partly through its own fault (especially the fault of Von Blomberg), partly through an astute policy on the part of Hitler. In February, 1934, Hammerstein was forced into retirement, and the defeat of the SA on June 30 of the same year proved to be a Pyrrhic victory for the generals. Not only did the SS succeed in getting rid of a rival and in extending its own hold, but Röhm's scheme of conquering the *Reichswehr* with a "people's army," that is, by a mass incorporation of the SA, was carried out by Hitler in a way but slightly different. The first step was taken in August, 1934, a few hours after the death of Hindenburg, when the *Reichswehr* was tricked into an oath of

[40] Fraenkel, *op. cit.*, pp. 202-3.

unconditional obedience to the Führer's person. This constituted a moral bond, however immoral in content, and an obstacle which, in accordance with all traditional standards, could not easily be overcome. The next step was the restoration of universal conscription in March, 1935. Beck, the successor and friend of Von Hammerstein, is on record as having opposed this measure, at least in its tempo and in its scope. He did so for technical as well as for political reasons. He foresaw not only a loss in quality and the dangerous trend toward bold adventures, but also the swamping effect as far as the anti-Nazi structure of the army was concerned.

In fact, the rapid increase opened the dike; it watered down army "separatism," which, however ambiguous in normal times, was an asset under circumstances as they then prevailed. It also opened splendid careers to young officers and unusual advancement to the higher ones. There is no doubt that Hitler's was a policy of deliberate bribery. While the very fact of the army's being the instrument of a criminal regime was in itself conducive of corruption, material temptation added greatly to the harmful effect. In many cases, "Prussianism" proved a hollow shell, just as the traditions of an austere past had vanished long ago among broad sections of the German people. In other words, officers were just as much infected by the poison of materialism which had spread since the late nineteenth century as were members of any other group. When generals had their *mésalliances* sanctioned, or their private debts settled, by the Führer—or, later on, were willing to receive large "personal" donations in money or estates from him—no link can be established between such an attitude and any militarist code or "categorical imperative" of an officer caste.

In addition, other factors worked against the resistance elements in the army. For one thing, Hitler's successes from the repudiation of the military sections of the Treaty of Versailles and the march into the Rhineland (March, 1936) through the annexation of Austria and the Sudetenland to the march into Prague (March, 1939), heightened his prestige. Having succeeded in one coup after another—and in all of them against the warnings of the army—he could assume an "I-told-you-so" attitude which undermined the credit of his opponents. Moreover, shortly before the march into Vienna, Hitler dealt the army a severe blow. In the course of a knavish intrigue, the compromised War Minister von Blomberg as well as the unimpeachable Commander in Chief von Fritsch were dismissed.[41] And on February 4, 1938, Hitler took unto himself the supreme command of the armed forces and established a new unified command *Oberkommando der Wehrmacht*, or OKW, under a typical yes-man (Keitel—or "Lackey-tel," as the resisters called him), who was made superior to the army Chief of Staff. At the same time a number of generals (ten to twelve commanders of corps and divisions), who had proved inaccessible—they were mostly bearers of old Prussian names—were also dismissed. It is less well known that this purge extended to about one hundred regimental commanders. Only one newspaper, in Silesia, dared to publish the list of the ousted men, and it was promptly suppressed as a result. The importance of this less conspicuous measure rests with the fact that regimental commanders decided on their own whether or not an officer candidate was to be accepted.

This was the situation when the war broke out. It explains something (though not all by far) of the defeat which the military part of the revolt suffered on July 20 at the hands of "loyal" officers; and it explains a good deal of the tantalizing story which unfolded through the years 1939-44. It was tantalizing from the viewpoint of those who urged military action, and it cannot fail to affect the historian, as an observer, with the same feeling.

A few remarks will suffice to characterize the "resistance against the resistance." Practically all witnesses, much as they differ in accent—Gisevius and Goerdeler, Hassell and Schlabrendorff—all

[41] For the shocking details, see the extensive story in Gisevius, pp. 219-65. A first-hand document of great value is the report of the chief of the juridical section of the army (*Wehrmachtsrechtsabteilung*), H. Rosenberger. It was first published in *Deutsche Rundschau*, LXIX (Nov., 1946), 8, and repeated by Pechel, *op. cit.*, pp. 141-47.

agree in their complaints about hesitancy and evasiveness on the part of army and army group commanders. Some could eventually be won over, as were Field Marshals von Kluge and Rommel; others had to be worked upon for months, only to slide back time and again. Whether this was due to conventional loyalty and misunderstood patriotism, or to faults of character, would have to be decided in each instance. The Captain of Reserves, Hermann Kaiser, who was attached to Colonel General Fromm, Commander of the Home Army, and who acted as an important liaison officer between Goerdeler and the military, noted in his diary on February 20, 1943: "the one is prepared to act upon order, the other to give orders when action has been taken."[42] This is probably as objective an analysis of the average military attitude as can be given. Most of the high commanders were likely to follow the lead if a break occurred—or better still, if the formal bond of the oath were removed by Hitler's assassination; but, while they did not wish to commit themselves, they were equally unwilling to denounce those who tried to persuade them[43]; nor did they feel very sure about what the young officers would do. The conspirators looked with contempt upon such an attitude. "These cowards make out of me, an old soldier, an anti-militarist," Von Hammerstein is said to have exclaimed.[44] Von Hassell spoke of the "hopeless sergeant majors."[45] And in the diary quoted earlier, Kaiser remarked: "One need only to think

[42] The one part of the Kaiser diary of which the manuscript has been preserved, covers the time from January 7 to August 3, 1943. It is supplemented by a fragmentary report of Ludwig Kaiser, who served as jurist on the staff of General Olbricht. Both brothers were in a position to record a good deal of the inside story. Hermann, a high-school teacher, deeply religious and an idealist of the purest type, fell a victim of July 20. A part of the fragment of the diary has been published in: *Die Wandlung*, 1945-46, Heft 5, pp. 530-34.

[43] An answer which seems typical came from Field Marshal von Kluge: 1. no participation in a failure; nor, 2. in an action against Hitler; but, 3. no obstacle in case action begins (Kaiser diary, Jan. 21, 1943).

[44] Dulles, *op. cit.*, p. 66.

[45] Von Hassell, *op. cit.*, p. 199. (The reference is to Von Brauchitsch and Halder on the occasion of Hitler's attack on Soviet Russia and his orders for a war of extinction.)

of a Scharnhorst, or Clausewitz or Gneisenau to realize to what level the officer of today has descended."

In Goerdeler's letters, the same indignation is strikingly voiced. To General Olbricht, Deputy Commander of the Home Army, who was in the plot from the beginning, he wrote on May 17, 1943, that it was not a matter of waiting for "the appropriate psychological moment," but of creating it.[46] A particularly bitter indictment he addressed to Field Marshal von Kluge, whose procrastinations were a major stumbling block. Goerdeler declared that he was no longer able to defend "Prussian militarism" against his friends, especially in southern Germany; these men "are in despair to think that with seeing eyes, a thinking brain, and a feeling heart one permits criminals and fools to lead the fatherland into an abyss and to drive German youth and German men into death and mutilation without doing something about it."[47]

Against this background there stand out the names of those professional soldiers who were determined to "do something about it." Beck, though retired, remained the acknowledged leader of the military Resistance. He came from a middle-class family in the Rhineland, a man of liberal traditions and a scientific bent of mind. He has been described as "combining the universal culture and the European scope of the eighteenth century with the basic principles of the Prussian past."[48] In fact, he recalls the forward looking generals and reformers of the years of 1807-1815, whose names were conjured up in Kaiser's diary. Rooted in a firm Christian faith, Beck was a military thinker of high caliber, and at the same time a student of contemporary problems beyond the professional sphere. Together

[46] Appendix to the Kaiser diary. The letter has been published in *Die Wandlung*, 1945-46, Heft 2.

[47] Appendix, *Ibid.*, July 25, 1943. The translation is taken from a manuscript of Louis P. Lochner, who used the same source. The German text is now printed in *Die Wandlung*, 1945-46, Heft 5, pp. 535-36.

[48] Marion Gräfin Dönhoff, *In Memoriam 20. Juli 1944* (Hamburg). The historian of the Prussian reform era, Friedrich Meinecke, who came into contact with Beck, calls him a "genuine heir to Scharnhorst" (*Die deutsche Katastrophe*, p. 146).

with three other members of the active political opposition (Popitz, Jessen, and Von Hassell), he belonged (as the only military man) to a group of civil servants and university people who gathered every Wednesday night in Berlin. As it happened, in one of the last meetings before July 20, Professor Heisenberg spoke of the philosophical implications of the physicist's new picture of the world.

There were other men of an unusual type among the military conspirators, such as Colonel Count Claus Schenk von Stauffenberg. After having been severely wounded, he became Chief of Staff of the Home Army in 1943, and thus obtained a key position; it was he who placed the bomb on July 20. A Catholic from Bavaria, a member of the circle of disciples around the German poet Stefan George, he was undoubtedly as much concerned about the cultural and religious as about the social and political implications of the Nazi Regime and of totalitarianism in general. If looks mean anything, his picture will make one realize that this was no ordinary colonel and no man of narrow military ambitions, however brilliant a soldier he had been.[49] In him, as in others, the intellectual clarity of the trained staff officer of the Prussian school blended with a purity and a spirituality which made him a natural leader in the fight against the dark forces of the age—against any kind of dehumanized policy in war or peace. Through his like-minded cousin, Count Peter Yorck von Wartenburg, he was closely linked with the Kreisau circle. He used to recite Stefan George's poem on the "Antichrist," in which the seer's eye, in an awesome vision, had forecast the things to come.[50]

[49] See the photograph in Schlabrendorff, between pp. 118-19. Stauffenberg's riends used to call him the "*Bamberger Reiter*," not only because he served in a Bamberg cavalry regiment, but also because of a striking resemblance to the famous Bamberg statue of the thirteenth century. Stauffenberg's portrait, as given by Karl Michel (*Ost und West: Der Ruf Stauffenbergs*, Zürich, 1947) is unfortunately obscured by a melodramatic emotionalism. A sound and documented study would be highly desirable. To the leading idea of Michel's book, reference will be made later on. The high tribute which the "SS Bericht" (see p. 10, n. 1) pays to Stauffenberg is of symptomatic interest, but obviously "second hand."

[50] Schlabrendorff, *op. cit.*, p. 66. The poem ("*Der Widerchrist*") in Stefan George, *Der Siebente Ring*.

But there were enough other officers who were soldiers first, and very much soldiers of the professional type.[51] Many were bearers of aristocratic Prussian names, and one could easily put together an impressive list of generals and of minor officers, from colonel down to lieutenant. A large number of them can be found on the honor roll of the victims of the Twentieth of July. Many of these officers held key positions. The deputy commander of the Home Army, General Olbricht, has already been mentioned. Field Marshal von Witzleben, as we saw, was ready to act in September, 1938, and never faltered. He was scheduled to take over the command of the armed forces after the removal of Hitler. In OKW Colonels von Freytag-Loringhoven and Hansen, in the Army High Command several heads of departments—Heussinger (?), Stieff, Wagner, Von Roenne, Fellgiebel, Lindemann—were members of the conspiratorial group. The commander of Berlin, Von Hase, was also in the plot, and Olbricht, together with the Colonels Mertz von Quirnheim and Wagner, worked on placing reliable men in command of other big cities. By the end of February, 1943, this process was completed. On the eastern front, the most important figure was Major General Henning von Tresckow, Chief of Staff for the Army Group Center. In the words of Schlabrendorff, his aide, "he threw every atom of his personality into our struggle,"[52] and he managed to assemble determined anti-Nazi officers around him, such as Von Kleist and Von Gersdorff, Count von Hardenberg and Count von Lehndorff. He also had confidants on the staff of the Army Group South. In the West, the commanders of the occupation armies were won over at an early date: in Belgium General von Falkenhausen, and in France General Count Heinrich von Stülpnagel, as well as members of his

[51] Ample evidence of the following can be gathered from Dulles and the various memoirs and diaries. A systematic survey, a sort of *ordre du bataille* in Pechel, *op. cit.*, pp. 337-38; *ibid.*, pp. 339-43, an honor roll, with about 140 names.

[52] *Op. cit.*, p. 30. Schlabrendorff (p. 22) makes it quite clear that Tresckow, a widely traveled man, was a determined anti-Nazi long before 1939. This might be compared with Gisevius' misleading statement (*op. cit.*, pp. 462-63).

staff and that of Rommel (General Speidel).[53] In fact, and para-doxically enough, the only complete overthrow of the Nazi power on July 20 occurred in Paris, where the arrests of Gestapo and SS men by Von Stülpnagel went off on schedule.

The question may then be asked why, in spite of such an array of key officers, all military plans of action eventually fell short of the mark. For one thing, it is true that the officers were poorly trained for conspiratorial work,[54] with the exception perhaps of those in the Intelligence Division. There was no revolutionary tradition extant in the Prusso-German army, such as exists in southern European countries or in Latin America. Another explanation suggests itself, and has been widely accepted: Nazi followers or vacillating non-Nazis foiled the attempts. There is truth in that, too. Much of the energy of the conspirators was consumed by the "labors of a Sisy-phus," as has already been stated. They never succeeded in winning over the head of the Home Army, Colonel General Fromm. And most of the active field commanders maintained a sort of neutrality. There were always some plausible arguments on hand. Could one risk having the stab-in-the-back legend turn like a boomerang against the officers' corps? As long as the road to victory still seemed open, how could one convince the people and the army that Hitler was leading them to disaster? And conversely, with the threat of defeat imminent, how could one precipitate catastrophe by breaking up the front? We saw that Goerdeler spoke derisively of the policy of "waiting for the appropriate psychological moment." In fact, this policy was an excuse for all sorts of weaknesses and ambitions.

But within the merely military circle of thought, there was hardly a way out of the impasse. And without having been faced with the same problem, one had better withhold generalizing judgments. It

[53] An eye-witness report on the events in Paris is found in: *Neue Zürischer Zeitung*, November 13, 1946. Lieutenant Colonel v. Hofacker, the conspirators' liaison man in Stülpnagel's staff, was a cousin of Von Stauffenberg.

[54] A small but significant incident is recorded by Meinecke (see p. 71, n. 48): Hermann Kaiser came to see him and to inquire about the organization of a conspiratorial German society of—1812-13.

required very strong convictions and a realization of a threat to the highest human values to break through the code of duty and patriotism to the point where one was prepared to revolt in the midst of an all-engulfing struggle, or eventually not only to wish and pray but also to work for the defeat of one's own country.[55] Some officers of high morality (for example, Von Fritsch or the German commander at Cherbourg) sought death on the battlefield as the only honorable solution of a bitter dilemma. The conspirators themselves naturally wanted to avoid a disastrous split of the army or a full-fledged civil war; they thought in terms of a "blitz revolution," to be carried out with a united armed force. Thus, a number of "psychological" moments—those before the attack on Norway, the Lowlands, and France, and those during and after Stalingrad—were squandered, as had been those which occurred before September, 1939.

But this is not the whole truth. In fact, many actions were planned although they lacked the support of high commanders. And the reason for their failure was not spineless neutrality, or the resistance against the resistance. When, in the summer of 1943, sealed orders were issued for "the day" (the code word being *Walküre*),[56] they assumed Hitler's death as a *fait accompli*. The orders provided for a state of "military emergency" (state of siege), during which the executive power would rest with the new Commander in Chief von Witzleben. It was then to be transferred to the commanders of the home front and of the occupied territories. SS troops were to be disarmed, and destroyed if necessary, concentration camps were to be seized, and so on. Of these orders, the one was signed by Witzleben

[55] A book that seems of great interest in this connection (Wolfgang Müller, *Gegen eine neue Dolchstosslegende*, Hannover, 1947) has become known to this author only through a review (*Der Kurier*, August 9, 1947). Müller represents the anti-Nazi and socially progressive officer at his best. As commander in Doeberitz (near Berlin), he was in the plot and took part energetically in the events of the Twentieth of July. But he also mirrors the typically military dilemma. And in his defense of the conspiracy against a new stab-in-the-back legend, he is not aware of the full length to which the leaders were prepared to go.

[56] Schlabrendorff, *op. cit.*, pp. 70-73.

"without hesitation." To the other Fromm's signature was "affixed without his knowledge"; it was signed by Stauffenberg. Whether or not this ruse might have worked, it certainly shows that no attention was paid to possible stumbling blocks. The same holds good for a number of attempts, which came close to execution, regardless of what the attitude of the neutrals would be.

The first one prepared to act (and to act at a moment of military triumph), was Von Hammerstein. During the Polish campaign he was commander of the German army on the Rhine. He succeeded in arranging for a visit by Hitler, and was determined to seize him upon arrival.[57] But the Führer had one of his "premonitions," the visit was cancelled, and Hammerstein was once more sent into retirement. He remained, however, a central figure of the conspiracy until his death in 1942. In a conference which took place in his home at the end of 1941,[58] and in which Beck and Goerdeler participated, an action was decided upon to be carried out by Witzleben, then commander in France. Pechel was sent to inform him, and Witzleben agreed to use his troops for the overthrow of the Nazi government. His staff was busy with preparations; but in March, 1942, Witzleben had to undergo an operation. One month later, Pechel was arrested, and the scheme broke down.

Initiative then shifted to the East. By this time the military had overcome the religious as well as the political objections which Goerdeler in particular had had against the plan of killing Hitler. He wanted instead to put him on trial. The soldiers, however, insisted that with increasing security measures, it was no longer possible to capture the Führer and that it was necessary to free the army of the oath. But they also knew that the initial spark had to be followed by a concerted military action, which was to be mapped out in every

[57] Dulles, *op. cit.*, p. 53; Schlabrendorff, *op. cit.*, p. 25; Pechel, *op. cit.*, p. 153. According to Pechel, Dr. Brüning called Hammerstein the only general who could remove Hitler—"a man without nerves." About another plot in November, 1939, see Dulles, *op. cit.*, pp. 54–55, and Kordt, *op. cit.*, p. 228.

[58] Pechel, *op. cit.*, pp. 155-56.

76

detail. This part of the task fell to Olbricht and his staff.[59] It has earlier been mentioned that he was ready by the end of February, 1943, and that sealed orders were issued that summer. The other part of the task fell to Tresckow. Failing to persuade Von Kluge, he decided to act on his own (though in close co-operation with Canaris of the Military Intelligence). After careful experiment, Schlabrendorff planted a time bomb in Hitler's plane on February 13, 1943, but it failed to explode.[60] A few days later, the attempt was repeated during the opening of an exhibition in the Berlin armory. According to the testimony of Von Gersdorff, who was another of Tresckow's associates, he carried two bombs in his pockets. But Hitler left the exhibition after eight minutes, while the delayed action fuses were set for twenty minutes.[61] Other attempts followed in spite of these disappointments and in spite of ever increasing measures for Hitler's protection. Schlabrendorff tells of a plan to shoot Hitler on sight.[62] Seven officers agreed upon it, but the Führer never again visited the Army Group Center. When, in December, Stauffenberg carried a bomb into the Führer's headquarters, the conference was canceled at the last moment.[63] Another opportunity seemed to arise in January, 1944, when Hitler was scheduled to inspect samples of a new uniform. Three young officers, one of them a son of Ewald von Kleist, were won over by Tresckow for the plot, and were ready to

[59] According to Schlabrendorff (p. 51), Olbricht, at the end of 1942, had asked for eight more weeks to perfect the plans for seizing power in Berlin, Cologne, Munich, and Vienna. At the end of February, 1943, he said: "We are ready; it is time for the spark." After the attempt of March 13, more complete measures were found necessary. This led to the sealed orders of Summer, 1943.

[60] Schlabrendorff, *op. cit.*, pp. 54-61.

[61] Pechel, *op. cit.*, pp. 162-64. According to Schlabrendorff (p. 61), the attempt had to be given up because a fuse was missing. There is, however, hardly any reason to doubt Von Gersdorff's detailed report, as recorded by Pechel.

[62] Schlabrendorff, *op. cit.*, p. 97.

[63] Dulles, *op. cit.*, p. 69. Gisevius (p. 473) speaks of another attempt at the end of 1943 which was organized by men in the Intelligence Division but failed because the explosives went off prematurely.

sacrifice their lives. But an air raid intervened, and the demonstration was indefinitely postponed.[64]

Eventually, in July, the final attempt was made by Stauffenberg, but it too stood under the star of misfortune. It was unfortunate, to begin with, that the "chief of staff" of the conspiracy had to set off the spark himself. He alone had access to headquarters. After having postponed his action twice, because of the absence of Göring and Himmler, he placed the bomb on July 20. But apart from other intervening circumstances—the conference had been shifted from the usual concrete shelter to a wooden barrack, a fact which fatally weakened the effect of the explosion and saved Hitler's life.[65]

In summing up this part of the story, one cannot avoid the conclusion that a number of failures were caused by an unbelievable accumulation of trivial incidents. Hitler might very well speak of "the hand of providence," and the historian may feel inclined to repeat this statement—not with the Führer's boasting note, but with a sense of reverence for the inexplicable. In the chain of events from 1933 to 1945 there seems to be a dire logic—an inner direction toward an unmitigated and inescapable catastrophe, which renders the incidental and the trivial significant.[66] And yet mishaps played an assignable role. They had something to do with Hitler's extreme caution, but nothing at all to do with caution, hesitancy, or lack of determination on the part of the officers concerned. And indeed, failure in itself has never been, or should never be, a final criterion of judgment.

But another critical question may be raised. What, even in the case of a successful "spark," could military resistance have amounted to? The answer is that in all essential features it was not exclusively

[64] Dulles, *loc. cit.* Pechel (*op. cit.*, pp. 164-66) and Schlabrendorff (*op. cit.*, pp. 99-100) have versions different in detail. Schlabrendorff (*loc. cit.*) reports another "unhappy accident" during a planned attempt at Berchtesgaden.

[65] Dulles, *op. cit.*, pp. 4-7.

[66] Edgar Salin, in an interesting article ("Die Tragödie der deutschen Gegenrevolution," *Schweizer Annalen*, II, N. 12, pp. 27-28), arrives at a similar conclusion. Differences between his and this author's interpretation will be indicated later on.

military at all. It had its motives as well as its aims in the political and moral sphere.

This study, therefore, is not concerned with the various oppositional moves against Hitler's strategic "intuitions," about the fatefulness of which Von Brauchitsch, Halder, Zeitzler, and many others were of the same opinion. They might speak indignantly of "that fellow," but theirs was no resistance in a fundamental sense. Nor do the various attempts to remove Hitler from the military command interest us here. Even a figure like General G. Thomas, Chief of the Production and Armament Division of the War Ministry, who was certainly in genuine opposition,[67] has only slight bearing upon our discussion. An expert in questions of military preparedness, he opposed Hitler's adventures from the beginning; in addition, he knew Russia well enough to side emphatically with Beck in the latter's somber predictions. As head of the economic branch of the army, he was in particularly close contact with civilian opponents;[68] he urged a number of generals early in 1940 to refuse to attack Holland and Belgium—the Berlin garrison then would arrest Hitler and the army take over. He continued to stress the necessity of ending the war, until his dismissal in late 1942. But his resistance, it seems, was one against a policy leading to defeat, rather than against the regime as such. And though his view that Hitler's assassination would make a martyr of him, and therefore should not be attempted, may be arguable, it is here that a fine dividing line appears.

Instinctively this line was drawn by Von Tresckow when he said in the summer of 1944:[69] "The assassination must be attempted, at any cost. Even should that fail, the attempt to seize power in the capital

[67] Cf. his report ("Gedanken und Ereignisse," *Schweizerische Monatshefte*, December, 1945, pp. 537-59).

[68] Material on this in Dr. Franz Reuter, *Der 20. Juli* (Berlin, 1946), pp. 10-14. Reuter was attached to the staff of General Thomas. The pamphlet, however, gives no more than generalities. (See also Pechel's criticism, *op. cit.*, p. 251.) For the following, some detail in Dulles, *op. cit.*, pp. 60, 65-66, 68; Gisevius, *op. cit.*, pp. 383-85, 447.

[69] Schlabrendorff, *op. cit.*, p. 103.

must be undertaken. We must prove to the world and to future generations that the men of the German Resistance movement dared to take the decisive step and to hazard their lives upon it. Compared with this object, nothing else matters." Of course, the military men who measured up to such a stature of opposition wanted also to avoid, if possible, bleeding Germany white, but they faced the issue as one threatening the whole world with chaos: as a profoundly moral issue. They felt, therefore, that the cleansing must be accomplished by their own efforts and, possibly, through their own sacrifices. We have seen that in the crisis of 1938 they opposed war not only because it would prove fatal to Germany, but because the imminent danger of war seemed to offer an opportunity to overthrow a criminal government and return to national as well as international standards of decency better in keeping with genuine military and truly noble traditions.

The same attitude continued to prevail through the war. It made a pale shadow of the specter of the "stab in the back" and of the accusation of high treason. When, after the failure of the Twentieth of July, Von Tresckow was prepared to take his life, his words of farewell to Von Schlabrendorff were:[70] "Everybody will now turn upon us and cover us with abuse. But my conviction remains unshaken—we have done the right thing. Hitler is not only the archenemy of Germany, he is the archenemy of the whole world. In a few hours' time I shall be before God answering for my actions and omissions." And he added: "Whoever joined the Resistance movement had to realize that his life was doomed. A man's moral value begins only when he is prepared to sacrifice his life for his convictions." Another of the military conspirators, Count Lehndorff-Steinort, wrote in his last letter to his wife:[71] "You must keep always in mind that I have not wantonly destroyed your future but have been serving an ideal that, I believe, does not allow consideration of family and private interests." The road to the Kingdom of Heaven, the

[70] *Ibid.*, p. 120.
[71] *Ibid.*, pp. 127-28.

letter continues, "maybe, must lead through sorrow, and every treasured possession must be forcefully torn away, since only thus can one become a 'new being'. . . . I shall die confident in this belief, without fear or doubt!"

These were some of the members of the "ambitious clique" who allegedly tried to get out of the war when it was lost in order to save themselves, or their caste or their class interests. Still more striking perhaps, and more contradictory to the picture of a Resistance composed of some disgruntled and "out-of-date" gentlemen, is the case of the German Military Intelligence (*Abwehr*). Its head, Admiral Canaris, foresaw at an early moment and as clearly as anybody else, the end to which a war of aggression would eventually lead. However, he felt that "an even greater misfortune would be the triumph of Hitler."[72] And he acted in accordance with this conviction. While his character is somewhat shrouded in mystery, his Chief of Staff, Major General Oster, stands out in clear profile: a man, says Schlabrendorff, "such as God meant men to be."[73] He not only furnished the conspiracy extensive cover and the most valuable liaison, he was also himself one of the driving wheels, and he did not shy away from taking action potentially detrimental to the German army. It has become known, beyond any doubt, that in advance of the invasion of Denmark and Norway, as well as that of the Lowlands and France, Oster gave the Dutch military attaché in Berlin details of the planned attack; and in the latter case, even the exact date. Previous to this, the General Staff had sent a secret warning to the Dutch minister in Berlin. It was transmitted through Count Albrecht von

[72] Dulles, *op. cit.*, p. 73 (based on the testimony of Major General Lahousen given at the Nuremberg trial). Much material on Canaris is to be found in Gisevius. It seems significant (both ways) that Sir Samuel Hoare in his memoirs (*Complacent Dictator*, p. 278), writes how surprised he was by the news "that Admiral Canaris . . . whose frequent visits to Spain had caused me so much anxiety, was one of the leaders of the movement." It seems also significant that the "SS Bericht über den 20. Juli" (see p. 10, n. 1) mentions Canaris' frequent conversations with Hoare. This is one more evidence of the fact that the Gestapo did not penetrate the secret.

[73] Schlabrendorff, *op. cit.*, p. 15.

Bernstorff, a former German diplomat who had resigned in protest to the regime.[74]

There seem to have been more such incidents. When recently a Canadian author, Major Milton Shulman, in his book, *Defeat in the West*, ascribed the failings of the German Military Intelligence to the "rigidity of the Teutonic mind," and insisted that the anti-Nazi feelings of the senior Intelligence officers had nothing to do with these blunders, an American critic who has been on the inside, remarked:[75] "We have chapter and verse on innumerable instances of this very type, involving not only deliberate garbling and misinterpretation of intelligence data but transmission to the allies of the most vital information. . . . " Here then, members of the General Staff, after having tried in vain to prevent war, worked to accelerate the defeat of their own country. Theirs was no narrow-minded traditionalism; nor did they skirt the dilemma.

It must be admitted that this analysis of the actions and attitudes of German military men does not exactly bear out some familiar ideas about "reactionary Junkers" and a "warmongering" General Staff. It may be that it lays open instead a very genuine, indeed the last great manifestation of "Prussianism" and of a Kantian "rigidity" of ethical standards which, one should wish, will never be "out of date". At any rate, the fault is not with the analysis or the facts referred to, but rather with some biased ideas. And it is not very flattering to state that these ideas coincide with the views which Goebbels held of the "blue blood," and also with Hitler's original estimate of the General Staff. During a visit to the Eastern front, he cried in an outburst of fury:[76] "Before I was head of the German Government I

[74] Dulles, pp. 58-60 (based on the statements of the Dutch Colonel G. J. Sas). The Bernstorff episode (November, 1939) accords with private information. Obviously the Gestapo got wind of the matter and Bernstorff was sent to a concentration camp. Freed by Halder, he continued his oppositional activities and was murdered by the SS in April, 1945 (see p. 32, n. 23).

[75] Prof. Harold C. Deutsch in: *Saturday Review of Literature*, January 17, 1948, p. 15.

[76] Schlabrendorff, *op. cit.*, pp. 34-35.

thought the German General Staff was like a butcher's dog—something to be held tight by the collar because it threatened to attack all and sundry. Since then I have had to recognize that the General Staff is anything but that. It has consistently tried to impede every action that I have thought necessary. It objected to the military occupation of the Rhineland, to the march into Austria, to the occupation of Czechoslovakia, and finally even to the war with Poland. It is I who have always had to goad on this butcher's dog."

While we then may conclude that the motives of the military opposition, as far as they concern us here, were not of a merely professional, and even less of a caste, character, the same clearly holds true for its aims. The Resistance movement in the army was a "sector," was part of a whole; and civilian aspects pervaded it from beginning to end. In this respect, it is worth mentioning that in the Staff of the Home Army and the Intelligence Services, where the number of conspirators was the largest, the number likewise of reserve officers and civilians was comparatively great. Lawyers, judges, teachers, professors, and churchmen had their part in the military planning: the Kaisers and Bonhoeffers, Justus Delbrück and Hans von Dohnanyi, Dr. R. Schleicher and Dr. Carl Sack, Freiherr von Guttenberg and Count von Schwerin-Schwanenfeld, Langbehn and Struenk. Moreover, co-operation between the military and the civilian sector was close. While in the deliberations of political circles, there were present representatives of Beck and Canaris (as will be shown by an example later on), rightist as well as leftist leaders conferred with and advised the military plotters. There were some civilians like Goerdeler and Von Hassell who constantly and desperately "prodded" the reluctant generals. There were others, it seems, who at times delayed rather than urged military action. According to one witness,[77] three of the younger socialist leaders, at the end of 1942, prevailed upon the military to postpone the attempt until the West-

[77] Emil Henk, *Die Tragödie des 20. Juli 1944* (Heidelberg, 1946), pp. 30-32. Inconsistencies appear, however, if one consults the military preparations (see p. 77, n. 59). See also Gisevius, *op. cit.*, p. 469.

ern allies had invaded the continent. Otherwise the overthrow of the government would only mean conquest by Russia and communism all over Europe. If this is a correct statement of the facts, it may to some extent explain a certain pause in military action between 1942 and 1943. At any rate, the international aspect came into consideration, as will be discussed later on. And this again points to the essentially political character of the military opposition.

Hence we may regard as perfectly true (though perhaps not exhaustive) the conclusion of Gustav Dahrendorf, one of the few survivors among the leading socialist conspirators:[78] "The revolutionary attempt of July 20, 1944," he said, "should not be considered as a badly managed undertaking by officers who had lost hope, and who wanted to escape from an awkward impasse; nor as an attempt of disgruntled, reactionary militarists to dissolve the link binding them to fascism. Both descriptions would be false and unjust. The motive force behind the preparations was a firm political will. *There was only one aim, to liquidate fascism and end the war.*" The military revolt, in fact, was only the first, though indispensable step toward this aim. It was "the spearhead of the Resistance Movement . . . neither its body nor its soul."[79] And a state of siege and of military control, though likewise indispensable, was thought of as a transitional measure only. In co-operation with the military, plans had been laid down for a new constitutional government, for the re-establishment of the rule of law, for freedom of religion, for political and social reforms.

It is to these aspects—to the political structure as well as the political aims of the Resistance—that our discussion must next turn.

[78] Schlabrendorff, *op. cit.*, p. 78.

[79] This sentence is taken from a very competent pamphlet of the "American Committee to Aid Survivors of the German Resistance" (145 East 52d Street, New York 22, New York).

Among the civilian leaders of the opposition, Carl Friedrich Goerdeler stands out most conspicuously. It is he, also, who has left behind various programs of action and reform for the post-Hitler regime. While they are not representative in any way of the whole of the Resistance movement, they give a basis at least for a preliminary appraisal of its ideas and aims.

Goerdeler had been mayor of Königsberg and commissar for price control under Brüning. In pre-Nazi days he excelled through a degree of personal initiative and political responsibility unusual for a civil servant. While elected lord mayor of Leipzig, he served for two years as price commissar under Hitler, trying in vain to put on the brakes. Like other impeccable foes of Nazism, he held it his duty not to retire at once, nor to leave the country; but on the other hand he refused to compromise his principles. Unable to prevent an anti-Semitic demonstration of the party in Leipzig (the removal of the Mendelssohn monument), he resigned his office in 1936. He then was employed in Stuttgart as an adviser to Robert Bosch, one of the most liberal and socially progressive German industrialists,[80] who provided him with the financial means and, still more important, with the necessary cover for his far-flung anti-Nazi activities. They extended practically to all noncommunist groups of the opposition, many of which found in him their rallying point. He was in contact with the military, of course, and with businessmen, with other retired civil servants and active members of the foreign office, but also with professors and churchmen (especially Archbishop Count von Preysing of Berlin and Protestant Bishop Wurm of Würtemberg), with trade unionists and socialist leaders. In addition, he had many friends

[80] On Bosch, see the recent biography by Theodor Heuss (*Robert Bosch, Leben und Wirken*, Stuttgart and Tübingen, 1946). The connection with Goerdeler was established by Th. Bäuerle (*op. cit.*, p. 674). More details on the Bosch circle in Frau Goerdeler's memorandum (see p. 57, n. 26), in Pechel (*op. cit.*, p. 209), and in a memorandum written by Bosch's private secretary (July, 1945).

abroad, and he traveled incessantly; through England and France, through Sweden and Belgium, through the Balkans and the Near East, through the United States and Canada. There is no doubt that in the years before the war, he did all in his power to make the outside world aware of what was in store and of the true character of the Nazi regime.

While in the United States in December, 1937, he left with one of his friends a "Political Testament."[81] It not only shows that he knew very well where he himself, and where the German people as a whole were heading. It also shows his primary alarm about lawlessness and corruption, about the breakdown of justice and the attack upon Christianity as the essence of a system that by foreigners was still being credited with some economic achievements. With his wide experience in administrative and financial matters, he was one of those "experts" who did not fall for the showy side of things. Long before the war (and even without a war) he was sure that Hitler would lead Germany into economic, and above all into moral, disaster. In his view, the German dictator throve upon the very disease that afflicted the age. In an article which Goerdeler published in the *Deutsche Rundschau* in April, 1938, he indicted materialism as the Great Error of our time. Liberation from this serfdom, he declared, could be won only through a "supreme effort of the moral forces which God has given men."[82]

In fact, it was from the angle of restoring basic human values, more than from any other, that Goerdeler began his agitation. He constantly tried to impress the generals with the danger of complete moral chaos if a regime of cynicism and criminal brutality continued, and he did not pass over their specific responsibility for this breakdown. They had looked on, he told them, while the principle of universal military service was deprived of its ethical content and made subservient to egotistic and criminal ends. Honor and decency, in

[81] Goerdeler's *Politisches Testament*, herausg. v. Fr. Krause, pp. 19-46. A "Program for the Peace of the World" (1938) is found, *ibid.*, pp. 47-52.
[82] *Ibid.*, pp. 53-55.

his view, were not "scrap iron"; they formed, instead, the core of any human institution, particularly one that demands supreme sacrifices. In a long memorandum which Goerdeler addressed on March 26, 1943, to a group of generals ("*An die Generalität*"),[83] he came to the conclusion that only one front was required in Germany: that of the decent versus the other people. And he asked the question which so often has been asked in foreign countries: How could the Germans (decent people in the main) endure such an unbearable regime? His answer was, because all violations of justice and decency are carried on under cover of secrecy and under terrorist pressure. What is practically necessary, he wrote, is to "restore a situation in which truth can be brought forth again, even if it were only for 24 hours." One may very well say that Goerdeler, though a man of broad practical knowledge, and thoroughly trained in the school of local self-government, was inclined to indulge in oversimplification and overoptimism. Time and again, his associates complained of these qualities in him. But nobody could (or can) deny that they had their roots in firm beliefs, in spiritual rather than materialistic beliefs, and proved an irrepressible driving force.

Another top figure in the civilian sector was the former ambassador to Rome, Ulrich von Hassell, who joined the active resistance after his dismissal in 1937. A son-in-law of Von Tirpitz, scion of an ancient Hannoverian family himself, he may be called a representative of the old elite—contemptuous of the upstarts, indignant at their stupid and arrogant blunders, a diplomat who lived in the genuine (as distinct from the distorted) tradition of Bismarck.[84] By his very

[83] Appendix to the Kaiser diary. A fragment is published in *Die Wandlung*, 1945-46, Heft 5, pp. 536-37.

[84] "It is regrettable," wrote Von Hassell, "what a false picture of [Bismarck] we ourselves have given the world—that of the power politician with cuirassier boots.... In truth the highest diplomacy and great moderation were his real gifts" (*The Von Hassell Diaries, 1938-1944;* with an introduction by Allen Welsh Dulles. New York, 1947, p. 353). See also the author's "Problems of a Bismarck Biography," *Review of Politics*, July, 1947. See also Von Hassell's caustic remarks on the launching of the battleship *Bismarck* and the refusal of his mother-in-law to christen the *Tirpitz* (*Diaries*, p. 35).

nature, Von Hassell was certainly as remote from a revolutionary or conspiratorial type as anyone could be. His diaries, surprising by their very existence as well as their preservation, show this amply. No Gestapo man would have had any trouble in converting them into plain language, and into a very telling story. But they also evidence Von Hassell's intellectual scope, the range of his activities through Germany and foreign countries (carried on, like those of Goerdeler, under cover of a business organization), his dealings with emissaries from abroad, and his contacts with oppositional elements which were by far not all members of an exclusive social circle.[85] Some of his ideas were admittedly of the past, and he was under some illusions, particularly in what he thought could be achieved by the foreign policy of the Resistance. To this international aspect our study will return.

It seems highly unjust, however, to point to Von Hassell, as American reviewers have done, as a specific example of a man "hopelessly out of date," "anachronistic in the modern world,"[86] or to speak flippantly of "high-minded Junkers who fought Hitler with 'diaries.'"[87] For one thing, an aristocrat (which Von Hassell was) who in the midst of a great world crisis reads Dante or Werner Jaeger's *Paideia*—a book that yields, as he says, "surprising insights into antiquity and the future"[88]—is perhaps not so "anachronistic" after all. To those who see an encouraging symptom in Europe's return to humanist and Christian traditions, he may instead appear as one more witness (among others) of the seeds which were sown in a time of chaos. Moreover, the diaries mirror, better perhaps than any other document, the motivating force which was alive in morally sensitive

[85] That Hassell had no contact with the Left and was "terrified" by the radical ideas of the younger generation (as Salin assumes; see p. 78, n. 66) is not borne out by the diaries (pp. 128, 131, 230-31, 283, 304, 315, 321). Hassell himself saw in Goerdeler, on the contrary, a sort of "reactionary" (pp. 214, 283). This controversy will be taken up later on.

[86] Ch. Poore in the *New York Times*, October 16, 1947.

[87] Peter Viereck, *ibid.*, November 30, 1947.

[88] *Diaries*, p. 319.

people of all classes, and which, after the completion of the catastrophe, American observers have often found to be missing: the consciousness of responsibility for shocking crimes carried out in the name of Germany and the urge to wash off the ignominy heaped upon her, not by diaries but by deeds. As far as Von Hassell was class-bound, he worked to make the sunken standard of *noblesse oblige* once more an effective force.

Other men of the old nobility were in the same camp: the former ambassador to Moscow, Count Werner von der Schulenburg; large landholders in Pomerania (the typical "Junker" province) such as Von Zitzewitz and Von Puttkammer, or a magnate in the Prussian province of Saxony, Wenzel-Teutschental, or Count Dohna-Tolksdorf. They had already opposed Hugenberg's course in pre-Nazi days. Prominent within the opposition of the landed gentry was Ewald von Kleist (the friend of Schlabrendorff), who in his trial before the People's Court in January, 1945, declared that he regarded his resistance "as ordained by God, and God alone should be his judge."[89] Again, this was not primarily a class movement (directed by "vested interests"), but one of individuals who were driven by genuine conservative principles and feelings of Christian piety.[90] Together with Goerdeler, other municipal officials, active and retired, should be named: his brother, treasurer in Königsberg, who joined him in the fate of execution as well as Drs. Elsas and Lehr; also jurists like Perels, the consultant of the Confessing Church, or the Catholic lawyers, Dr. Wirmer and Joseph Müller. In addition, one or the other of these loosely knit groups included men who had been active in the direction of Liberal-Conservative, Democratic, and Centrist policies (Lejeune-Jung, a former Reichstag deputy; Gessler and Hermes, former ministers; Bolz, a former state president,); likewise a number of civil servants in retirement, (an *Oberpräsident*, the Catholic Baron von Lüninck, and two former secretaries of the chancellery,

[89] Schlabrendorff, *op. cit.*, p. 139.
[90] See Lysbeth W. Muncy, "The Junkers and the Prussian Administration from 1918 to 1939," *Review of Politics*, October, 1947, pp. 499-500.

Hamm and Planck, among them). Other members of the same circles have been mentioned before, and more names could be added to the list of prominent civilians.

One of these, the Prussian Minister of Finance Johannes Popitz, merits a few additional remarks because of the controversial character of his activities. As a theorist and practical administrator, he had won a brilliant reputation during his early service under the Socialist Minister of Finance, Hilferding. He joined the Nazi government as an expert, soon to be disillusioned. That he was, at least since 1938, a bitter enemy of the regime, and deeply concerned about the spread of corruption, is incontestable. A man of personal integrity and high intelligence, an archaelogist and political scientist in his own right, and a member of the Wednesday Society, he came early to the conclusion that the war was lost and that under Hitler's and Ribbentrop's direction no peace could be reached. He participated in the attempts to forestall the attack in the West in 1940;[91] he was more or less closely connected with Hassell and Schacht, Oster and Gisevius.[92] With Goerdeler, however (whom he is said to have called ironically a "country pastor" and a "political traveling salesman"), he fell out, over differences in social and political concepts.[93] These differences (roughly those between Goerdeler's more "liberal" or "parliamentary" and Popitz' more "bureaucratic" or "authoritarian" views) will be referred to later on. Certain it is that Beck, Goerdeler, and the trade-union leaders distrusted Popitz because of his active part in the regime and his party membership, while his preference for a planned economy of a sort and for state-socialist measures seem to have made him more acceptable to men of the younger generation, that is to the Kreisau circle.

[91] Dulles, *op. cit.*, p. 153; Hassell, *op. cit.*, pp. 101, 113.

[92] Gisevius (*op. cit.*, p. 432) gives the impression that he found "Popitz' case ... far more crass than the 'ambiguous' case of Schacht"; that he himself "vetoed" Popitz emphatically, but was won over by his manifest sincerity. Whatever this statement may be worth, Gisevius knew very little of Popitz' activities.

[93] Dulles, *op. cit.*, pp. 155-56. For the following, see Dulles, chapter XI (Himmler).

At any rate, Popitz convinced himself that the generals would not act ("they think only of their medals"); in despair, it would appear, he hit upon the idea of a "palace revolt" or a revolt among the "pretorial guard"—which indeed are, next to a military putsch, the two other typical ways out of a dictatorship. After having tried, with occasional success, to bring Göring under his influence, he turned to Himmler, who since 1943 had been Minister of the Interior. When Mr. Dulles moved into Germany, Miss Marie-Louise Sarre, an active member of the conspiratorial groups,[94] informed him of Popitz' ideas. He also had the good fortune of finding somewhere "along the railway tracks" the indictment which was prepared for the trial of Popitz and his adviser, the lawyer Dr. Langbehn. Whatever the value of this lengthy document, together with the Sarre testimony it reveals beyond doubt that Popitz had a conversation with Himmler in August, 1943. It moved cautiously round the problem of "reducing the power of the Führer." From other sources it is known that in the last phase, Himmler, in fact, was on both sides of the fence.[95] This, however, is not a subject pertaining to our study. Indeed, as far as the genuine Resistance is concerned, accidental evidence should not induce us to place too much emphasis on the Popitz-Himmler episode. It was an action distinctly out of line. Beck and Goerdeler, though they might have welcomed an open split in the Nazi front, were in no way involved in the approach to Himmler.[96] In summing up, one may credit Langbehn as well as Popitz with personal courage and specifically with saving the life or liberty of a number of people, toward whose protection they used their access to Göring and Himmler. Their separate actions, however,

[94] Pechel (*op. cit.*, p. 227) depicts her as the "blonde angel" of the prison in Ravensbrück. She was a sister-in-law of Eduard Waetjen, a friend of Von Moltke, who was attached to the German consulate in Zürich, and, next to Gisevius, served as a link between Mr. Dulles and the Underground.

[95] A detailed analysis of this phase has been given by H. R. Trevor-Roper, *op. cit.*

[96] Besides the evidence in Mr. Dulles' chapter, see Hassell, who seems to have heard of the approach only after Langbehn's arrest. He speaks of "a growing tendency of important groups to reject Popitz" (*op. cit.*, p. 321).

were bound to fail. It took Bormann, the chief of the party and rival of Himmler, only a month to get wind of the matter. Both Popitz and Langbehn fell as victims of an intrigue within the pretorial ranks, rather than as members of the conspiracy.[97]

Nor can Schacht be included in the group of the civilian leaders. He was certainly very active in opposition since 1936, increasingly so after his dismissal in January, 1939; a top figure as far as intelligence and contacts are concerned. But a marked record of ambition, vanity, and opportunism prevented his being admitted to full partnership.[98] Like Gisevius, who seems to have been the one nearest to Schacht, he was kept at arm's length by the leaders of the conspiracy. As far as sources permit such a distinction to be made, he was not present at any of the quasi-official meetings of the conspirators. Nor was he scheduled for a place in the "shadow government."

It is different with the key conspirators of the Left; these had an equal share in the preparation of the coup as well as in the responsibilities to be assigned after the overthrow of the regime.

Prominent among the leaders of labor was Wilhelm Leuschner, a former Minister of the Interior in Hesse and head of the socialist ("Free") Trade Unions since 1932. After two years in a concentration camp, he established a small factory in Berlin, which gave him not only his livelihood and funds for agitation, but an excellent cover for employing a cadre of reliable social-democratic workers. He traveled as an inconspicuous businessman, or sent out "salesmen" acting as agents to reinstitute contacts between the cells of the trade unions, or even with the International Labor Organization. The factory produced a special sort of beer faucet, which was invented by

[97] Accordingly, the facts as given by Dulles, *op. cit.*, pp. 162-64, are of interest mainly for an understanding of the Gestapo and party atmosphere. There is, however, no chapter "Himmler" in the history of the German Underground, as the arrangement of the material in Mr. Dulles' book would suggest.

[98] See Hassell (*op. cit.*, p. 215, September, 1941): "Apparently Schacht sees things very clearly, but his judgment is always affected by his boundless personal ambition and his unreliable character." That Schacht played no part in the Putsch is also the opinion of the "SS Bericht" (see p. 10, n. 1).

Schneppenhorst, also a trade-union leader and a victim of the Twentieth of July. In this article, the military began to show an unusual interest. General Beck, we are told, "disguised by blue glasses, was a frequent visitor at the factory."[99] Olbricht, according to Pechel,[100] provided the traveling salesmen with special papers. Leuschner himself, by profession a sculptor in wood, skillful and tenacious, must have instilled confidence in all who came into contact with him, and who struck in him a responsive chord. His code name was "uncle," and Von Hammerstein, the "Red General," addressed him as an old friend.

In fact, the relations between trade unionists and military or even conservative circles went back to the pre-Hitler era. Erwin Planck, the son of the famous physicist and Secretary of the Chancellery under Schleicher, had worked for such a front, and may have been active again as a liaison man along the same line.[101] With Goerdeler, also, a close co-operation was soon established. Pechel relates that he arranged for an initial meeting of Goerdeler with Leuschner and his associate Hermann Maas, the former chairman of the socialist youth organizations. A common platform was found—obviously not one with just the negative purpose of overthrowing the regime, but one based on similar convictions, on mutual esteem and absence of personal ambition, and apparently also on a considerable area of agreement regarding positive political and social aims. Hassell defined this rapprochement in his own terms when he noted[102] that Leuschner and his friends "are thinking along clearly national and religious lines" and that "important elements of the former Social Democratic party share these views."

[99] Dulles, *op. cit.*, p. 106. According to Henk (*Die Tragödie des 20. Juli 1944*, p. 12), the navy was interested in one of Leuschner's articles, and Canaris used this connection as a bridge to socialist circles.

[100] *Op. cit.*, p. 202.

[101] Partly on personal information. Because of Planck's incessant activity and devotion, Hassell (p. 204) called him the "circuit preacher." He was executed in January, 1945. The text of a memorial sermon could be used.

[102] *Op. cit.*, p. 304 (June, 1943).

The religious note in the oppositional front was naturally strongest among the Christian trade unions. Their leader, Jakob Kaiser, had also been close to Von Hammerstein, and had worked in association with Dr. Brüning in the pre-Hitler days. He was linked with men like Bernhard Letterhaus, a former member of the Prussian Diet, and Nikolaus Gross, a former miner, with Heinrich Koerner and Franz Leuninger, all having been active in Catholic labor organizations. Backed by the prelate Dr. Müller in Cologne and the student pastor in Berlin, Dr. Schmitt, these men worked together to build their own cells of resistance.[103] Common ground with Goerdeler was easily found, and there is no indication that it was more difficult to come into close contact with Leuschner's circles either. The situation differed from what it had been in the early years, and what it continued to be among the *émigrés*. At least within the trade-union camp, old boundary lines lost their meaning; to fight any totalitarianism was a common concern of Catholics and Socialists. It may be mentioned that Jakob Kaiser, one of the few survivors of the conspiracy, has upheld this front as leader of the Christian Democratic Union in the Russian zone —until, quite recently, he was ousted under Soviet pressure.

The same front[104] was joined by Max Habermann, the former head of the white-collar workers' union, which had had rightist leanings. He was a personal friend of Goerdeler, sometimes staying with him in Leipzig[105] and keeping up a cadre of his organization.

While the trade unionists provided the conspiracy with a network of functionaries, who might often be the same as those of the socialist underground, and with a shadow apparatus (in this being comparable to the Intelligence Service), some individual Socialists contributed a more strictly political impulse. There were men who had been connected with Leuschner before: Ludwig Schwamb and Dr.

[103] For personal details, see Pechel, *op. cit.*, pp. 201-7. Pechel's connections with Dr. Müller and Dr. Schmitt are one more evidence of the inter-confessional front.

[104] According to Henk (*op. cit.*, p. 22), a unified bloc of all three trade unions was agreed upon as a program for the future.

[105] According to Frau Goerdeler's memorandum.

Carlo Mierendorff, the one a state councillor, the other a Reichstag deputy in Hesse. Mierendorff, in general estimate, was one of the most vital and brilliant foes of the regime, highly intellectual and at the same time a full-blooded personality and a born popular leader.[106] For more than four years he had been in a concentration camp. Upon his release he joined in clandestine activity with his friend, Dr. Theo Haubach, the former editor of a Hamburg socialist paper, and also a concentration camp "alumnus" (Dulles). Mierendorff had connections with Canaris and was an important member of the Kreisau circle. Haubach also belonged to this circle, as did Adolf Reichwein,[107] who until 1933 had been a professor at a teachers' college. He was particularly active in adult education, a Marxist and a follower of Grundtvig at the same time. These men cannot be called "rightist" Socialists; they were, culturally speaking, "conservative"—that is, seriously concerned about the preservation of creative religious and artistic forces in the lives of the people. They were outright radicals in social and political matters—all three presenting this not unusual combination at its best. It was a severe loss for all oppositional groups when Mierendorff was killed in an air raid on Leipzig in December, 1943. Dr. Julius Leber succeeded him as a potential leader of the radical wing. Four and a half years of brutal treatment by the SS had not broken his will; and with politics as his true passion, he soon entered the vanguard of the conspiracy. Through Dahrendorff and Ernst von Harnack, he established contact with Goerdeler[108] and completed the roster of men able and destined to take over as soon as the military blow should fall.

Preparations for this moment had advanced with the years, and had

[106] See the portrait of Mierendorff (and Haubach) as sketched by Zuckmayer; reprinted in *Deutsche Innere Emigration*.

[107] A commemorative article on Reichwein and his pedagogic activities by A. v. Machui in: *Die Sammlung*, October, 1945.

[108] Pechel, *op. cit.*, p. 204. Mr. Sulzberger's statement that "only the rather Rightist Socialists played an active part" is one of the many errors his article contains (see p. 59, n. 31). See also *Neue Volkszeitung* (February 21, 1948) and its attack on a "new legend" destined to minimize the part of the Left.

gone farther than has often been realized. There would have been no vacuum, had the Hitler regime ended on July 20—nothing of that deadly unpreparedness that, by contrast, prevailed in May, 1945. Of course, there were differences between the top civilians: differences in opinion and differences in personal matters. The latter were gradually adjusted, and need not be considered here.[109] It may suffice to point out the result. In early 1944, a sort of shadow government was agreed upon. Beck was to be provisional Chief of State, Goerdeler Chancellor, and Leuschner Vice-Chancellor, with Jakob Kaiser as his deputy. The Ministry of Foreign Affairs was assigned to Hassell (with Von der Schulenburg as alternate), the Ministry of War to either Olbricht or Oster, with Stauffenberg as Undersecretary and Witzleben as Commander of the armed forces. The important Ministry of the Interior (important particularly because it included control of police) was to go to Leber, who would thus hold a key position. It is significant also that for the Ministry of Information, another Socialist, Haubach, was chosen. The Ministry of Reconstruction was assigned to the Catholic labor leader, Letterhaus, that of Economics to Lejeune-Jung, and that of Culture (after Popitz had been dropped) to Bolz. The Ministry of Justice was to go to Dr. Wirmer, that of Finance to Loeser, a former mayor of Leipzig, who as a director general of Krupp had joined the opposition. Governors with clear anti-Nazi records (Gessler, Steltzer, and Von Lüninck, for example) were chosen for the German states, and mayors of similar character for the larger cities.

If one examines this roster of personnel, it seems at first sight to resemble one of the coalition governments of the Weimar days—with a military "whale-bone" as its proper support. But the differences from the pre-1933 era cannot be overlooked. For one thing, the various component elements of this coalition had come to know and appraise each other the hard way. None of them represented the ordinary type of the ambitious politician, or was forced to appease

---

[109] Gisevius, *op. cit.*, p. 487. For some details, see Henk, *op. cit.*, pp. 34-36. For the roster, see Dulles, *op. cit.*, pp. 180-81, and the "SS Bericht über den 20. Juli."

the susceptibilities of outworn parties. Moreover, they all were aware of the fact that they were risking their lives for the sake of their convictions—a fact which makes for a specific selectivity in bringing forth leadership. This sort of "elite" was bound to be one of character rather than of social rank or political standing. Hassell might very well speak of a "Band of Brothers" (December, 1943).[110] Whether or not they agreed in opinions, they had ground in common which recalls Goerdeler's "front of decency."

At any rate, the composition of the shadow government may definitely dispose of the legend which has characterized the conspiracy as one of out-of-date gentlemen, disgruntled generals, and reactionary civilians who gathered only because, or became articulate only when, "the war was completely lost."[111] Yet another question remains regarding the political structure of the opposition. How far did it extend through the country? How far did it reach down, not only to loosely organized circles, but to the masses of the German people? In other words: Was not the Resistance floating in the air, headed for failure, even if the military putsch should succeed?

In answering this, two aspects may be distinguished: that of the existence of a certain amount of mass opposition, and that of the links between the "elite" and the broader oppositional moves.

Paul Maerker, a former German trade-union leader and himself a prominent underground member in the first years of Nazi rule, puts the number of workers organized in an anti-Nazi front at about 125,000—that is, 3 per cent of those who had belonged to the Free Trade Unions prior to 1933. And he adds that these groups were completely taken by surprise on July 20: "No preparations were made for striking together with the generals."[112] This is certainly true in

[110] Op. cit., p. 327.

[111] As late as September, 1947, Karl Loewenstein has repeated this view and criticized Allen W. Dulles' book as "wholly misleading"(!) (Social Research, XIV, 365). This criticism is all the more untenable, since Mr. Dulles' book gives little interpretation, but a large amount of solid facts.

[112] Quotation from The Christian Science Monitor, January 8, 1945, p. 7, col. 1.

the sense that no warning of imminent events was given in advance. Nor could it be given; not even the leading civilians were on the inside. But the existence of a network of cells is undeniable. In addition to what has been previously said, in a general way, about the new tactics of the illegals since 1935, more specific evidence can be quoted. In 1942 a French worker, who came back from Germany, stated somewhat summarily that in every factory "4 or 5 men belong to the organized socialists." The others, he thought, sympathized with this cell.[113] More convincing perhaps is the "conservative" estimate (as the authors expressly say) of the United States Bombing Survey report, which stresses the following facts:[114] "In 1944 approximately one of every 1,200 German adults was arrested by the Gestapo for a political or religious offence. Organized opposition groups were found in most German cities." Moreover, the American investigators stated that, although "activities were normally confined, by necessity, to a local scale," there were also "efforts on a national scale" carried out by Trade Unionists, Socialists, and Communists.

While it can be safely assumed that men like Leuschner, Kaiser, and Leber (and churchmen as well) had their part in these efforts, it would appear that the conspiratorial groups developed their own system of links. As Professor Alfred Weber, of Heidelberg, said to an American correspondent:[115] "Thousands, literally thousands, of civilians were involved in the assassination plot." This is borne out by definite indications. When in May, 1942, two pastors of the Confessing Church approached the Bishop of Chichester in Stockholm, they informed him of the character of the German opposition in a

[113] W. W. Schütz, *German Home Front*, p. 165. A "Report on the 20th of July, 1944" (edited by the Executive of the Social-Democratic Party of Germany, residing in London), which was based on reports of a recent refugee, estimates that "the number of conscious anti-Nazis amounts to 35 to 40%. The largest portion is made up by the Social-Democratic workers. But they include also many intellectuals of widely differing political views."

[114] *Op. cit.*, I, 2, 101-2.

[115] According to Joel Sayre, *New Yorker*, August 11, 1945, p. 63. See also Gabriel A. Almond, who after using 'some Gestapo files (p. 14, n. 10) concludes: "The actual resistance was larger and more varied than indicated."

way, which in general can be proved to be perfectly correct. One of their statements was that "through a network of key men systematically developed during the last six months" the trade-unionist members of the conspiracy controlled "key positions in the main industrial centers as well as in the big cities like Berlin, Hamburg, Cologne, and throughout the whole country."[116] It is impossible, of course, to check this assertion in detail. But the description fits in with that which the Socialist Henk has given.[117] He credits Leuschner, in particular, with building up an "invisible net" all over Germany. And regarding one specific district (Kassel-Heidelberg), he outlines an organization of key men, each of whom, in his words, was to be responsible for mobilizing ten to twenty more anti-Nazis at a given moment. The names which Henk lists cover not only sizable towns, but also smaller communities down to the villages. His estimate is that in the one region alone, ten to fifteen thousand men stood prepared for action on July 20.

Whether or not this description can be fully accepted and generalized, it still does not imply a mass organization. For obvious reasons no attempt of this sort could be made. And as the military putsch failed, the key men on the local level were not called up either. But it seems to be an established fact that, whatever the details, the plot reached much farther down than has often been believed. One should therefore no longer talk about its "rootless character." In addition, there is little doubt that, in 1944, the masses of silent opponents, this broad potential of resistance under any totalitarian regime, would have turned against their oppressors, once the clutches of the Nazis were broken.

Such an assumption is not contradicted by the fact that no spontaneous uprising against the party bosses occurred when the Allies marched in.[118] Conditions were very different after another year of bombing, that is, after an unimaginable amount of physical and mor-

---

[116] The Contemporary Review, CLXVIII, 203.
[117] Op. cit., pp. 48-51.
[118] This argument has been used by Loewenstein, op. cit.

al destruction, and at a time when "liberation" was coupled with "conquest."

But the perspective of a broader revolutionary movement and the mass support upon which the left wing of the coalition could probably count, brings up other problems: Was there a basic political unity beyond the common moral convictions and the "one aim to liquidate fascism and end the war"? Was there a stock of ideas which could carry over from the mere establishment of a post-Hitler government into constructive action? Was there a chance for political and social democracy to take root? Or was the coup d'état bound to be an episode, because of the inner dissent between "conservative" and "radical" tendencies, or because of the "natural" dynamics of revolutionary movements?

These are speculative questions to which, of course, no definite answer can be given. But material is available which seems interesting enough to warrant a brief discussion and which permits us at least to clarify the issues involved.

5

Constitutional and Social Ideas

Goerdeler, most active in conspiratorial work, was also most active in planning for the future. He has set down more or less elaborate proclamations, programs, and outlines. But he did so not entirely on his own. Many conferences were held with Beck, Hassell, and Popitz, with members of the churches and the younger men of the Kreisau circle; that there were none with Kaiser and Leuschner is altogether unlikely. According to Goerdeler's widow,[119] one result of the conversations with labor leaders was a book ("Primer of Economics") which he wrote in the last two years of his life, and which was meant to enable the workers to take more interest and a more active part in the management of "their" factories. Though

[119] Her memorandum has been used for the following. For additional information, see Dulles, *op. cit.*, p. 122, and Pechel, *op. cit.*, pp. 105-6, 210-13.

one would miss the point in calling Goerdeler "a man of the people," he was certainly socially minded in a sincere and genuine way. And it stands to reason that something of the spirit of the Bosch concern, in which the workers were made to feel themselves as responsible partners, had colored his thought. It is possible that he may also have been influenced by the example of the even more progressive Zeiss plant in Jena.

In connection with Goerdeler's preparations, one should also mention some of the writers and professors who were members in various degrees of the political opposition. Pechel framed one draft of a public appeal, Hermann Kaiser another. The jurists Rudolf Smend and Dr. Goetze-Jena worked on legal questions. Particularly active was a group of political scientists, economists, and historians at Freiburg University: Eric Wolf, Adolf Lampe, Constantin von Dietze, Walter Eucken, Gerhard Ritter. They all belonged to the Confessing Church, and it seems that Pastor Bonhoeffer established their contact with Goerdeler. Here again the basis of co-operation was one beyond mere politics. Professor Albrecht-Marburg was also consulted in economic matters and Professor Litt-Leipzig in educational questions. Thus a considerable body of thought could be assembled.

The first program we know of is the very sketchy one of January-February, 1940.[120] It was written by Hassell in co-operation with Beck, Goerdeler, and Popitz. It was meant to be used in case the opposition against the attack in the West resulted in the hoped-for overthrow of the regime. The program provided for a regency, composed of three members appointed to stay in power until "normal constitutional life" could be re-established. The task of preparing for this moment fell to an appointive Constitutional Council, while the executive power lay with the Chief of the Regency (Beck?), and was to be delegated to military district commanders. A state of siege seemed indispensable, if chaos were to be averted and the "dignity of law" to be restored, in contrast to the moral devastation which had resulted from the previous regime. The fatal balance sheet of the Nazi rule,

[120] Hassell, *Diaries*, pp. 368-72.

as well as the first countermeasures to be taken, were briefly outlined.

It seems that Goerdeler thought of basing the interim government at once upon popular support. He wanted to have "a plebiscite immediately,"[121] a plan which recalls his belief that the whole situation would change, if truth could "be brought forth again even if it were only for 24 hours." But his optimism was not shared by others. In additional drafts, Jessen outlined rules for the state of siege (which are said to have been very stringent), and Popitz mapped out an ordinance "for the restoration of lawful procedures in political and juridical life"—that is, a "preliminary constitutional law." It put great emphasis both upon purification and future effectiveness of the civil service, and was scheduled to remain in force until "with co-operation of all elements of the German people a definite constitution can be set up."[122]

As to the executive power, Goerdeler and his friends considered for some time the idea of a monarchical restoration. What they wanted was to place the highest authority as "a firm central pillar" (Popitz) outside and above shifting opinions and party pressure. And in view of the experiences of the Hitler regime, when the climax of totalitarianism was reached with the merging of the positions of party head and chief of state, something could be said for this idea. An old democratic, south-German minister of the Weimar days, Gessler, advocated a Wittelsbach restoration.[123] Just as National Socialism had its origins in Austria and Bavaria, monarchical legitimism had

[121] *Ibid.*, p. 109 (January, 1940), also p. 231 (December, 1941). The Gestapo also held the view that Goerdeler "envisaged a system of popular representation," while Popitz rejected this as impossible (Dulles, *op. cit.*, p. 155).

[122] Some of the drafts are in U. v. Hassell, *Vom anderen Deutschland*, pp. 385-96 (these appendices are left out in the American translation). Jessen's draft has not been found, but can be reconstructed to some extent on the basis of Popitz' "rules of application." Popitz' preliminary constitutional law has been preserved in a draft of 1943, but seems to go back to January, 1940. In its qualified centralism it mirrors ideas of the Weimar era, which Popitz had set forth as early as 1929 (*Volk und Reich*, Berlin, 1929, II, 328-62). Hassell, not unjustly, found that Popitz' plans were "too strongly influenced by the requirements of administrative efficiency and too little by political sensitivities" (*Diaries*, p. 109, January, 1940).

[123] Hassell, *Diaries*, p. 128.

its strongest roots in the South. And Bavarian members of the conspiracy were likely to favor Rupprecht, heir of the Wittelsbach line. Another candidate was the Hohenzollern ex-Crown Prince Wilhelm, who declared himself "ready to step into the breach and assume all sacrifices and dangers—about the extent of which he had no illusions."[124] More suitable, however, seemed to be his second son Louis Ferdinand, who was known to be a favorite of Queen Mary, and who had worked for some time as a mechanic in the United States. As to the reaction in America, Hassell was assured by an American businessman that such a choice "would be downright popular".[125]

One can, of course, doubt very much that this was a true prediction, even before Pearl Harbor. But it would be hasty to characterize these plans as essentially antidemocratic. They were patterned after the English model, and pointed toward a monarchical presidency within a parliamentary system. Goerdeler, least of all his associates among the older generation, favored anything like the restoration of the old power of the Prussian monarchy. He is said to have expressly stated that the President (whether monarch or regent) "is not meant to govern but to watch over the constitution and to represent the state."[126] And about one thing there was full agreement: nothing in the new regime should recall a "Kapp Putsch." The military themselves, Hammerstein and Beck above all, insisted on that. And of the group of younger men forming the Kreisau circle, Trott zu Solz impressed Hassell with the necessity of avoiding "any semblance of 'reaction', 'gentleman's club,' 'militarism'" (December, 1941).[127] It

[124] Ibid., p. 202 (July, 1941).

[125] Ibid., p. 214 (September, 1941). Hassell's diaries use "Stallforth" as a pseudonym for this businessman.

[126] Gerhard Ritter, "Goerdelers Verfassungsplane," Nordwestdeutsche Hefte, I, No. 9, Dec., 1946, p. 12.

[127] Hassell, op. cit., pp. 230-31. Trott's candidate for the chancellorship, incidentally, was Dr. Niemöller. Hassell mentions (ibid.) that Goerdeler insisted on his "good relations with the Social Democrats" and that he (like Beck) was less positive regarding the Crown Prince. Neither his name, nor Louis Ferdinand's, recurs in the Diaries after December, 1941. In the indictment of Popitz and Langbehn, it is also stated that "the other conspirators rejected the possibility of a monarchy" (Dulles, op. cit., p. 154).

was by this time, as far as we can see, that the monarchical idea disappeared altogether.

Of greater interest is Goerdeler's constitutional planning.[128] The underlying concept was a high evaluation of self-government. This implied decentralization (federalism) on the one hand, and on the other hand electoral modes destined to bring men into politics who had already won their spurs in local or professional affairs, and were well known to their constituencies. Thus, Goerdeler wanted to go back to the sound German traditions of a time when politics had not yet been mechanized and dehumanized. Moreover, to make parliament capable of responsible action, Goerdeler suggested restricting the parties to three. For the same reason he wanted to follow the British example of allowing only for personal candidatures (instead of "lists") and for decision in one ballot by simple majority. But only one half of the popular chamber was, in this plan, to be elected directly on the basis of universal suffrage; the other half was to be elected indirectly in a sequence of ascending stages, starting from the local representation. Deputies of the Reichstag were required to be at least thirty-five years of age, and to have served five years in local government. They should also be residents of their constituencies. It is obvious that all this meant a preference for the administrative and local as against the strictly political element. In addition, Goerdeler planned an upper chamber composed of representatives of the great occupational units, of the associations of employers, of the *one* trade union, of churches and universities; a chamber including also fifty freely appointed "distinguished Germans of all classes." In order to guarantee a stable government, the Reichscabinet was not to be removable by a simple vote of non-confidence, but only by a qualified majority of the popular chamber, or the consent of both houses.

All these were not yet definite, and by no means accepted, plans of

[128] The main body of information is drawn from Gerhard Ritter's article, *op. cit.* The publications in *Neue Zeitung* (February 1, 4, 8, 1946) and *Gegenwart* (12-13, 1946), were not available.

the Resistance. But they point significantly toward a conservative system of checks. Goerdeler certainly "went back," for example, to the ideas and the work (especially the town ordinance) of the great German reformer, the Freiherr vom Stein[129] (while not sharing the latter's merely historic preference for the propertied classes), and to his own practical experiences in the administration of large self-governing cities. But to return to valuable traditions does not necessarily imply "reactionary romanticism." It has been attested (by Pechel) that Goerdeler was constantly growing in stature, a man of increasing receptivity. In fact, his ideas underwent a considerable development. As Jakob Kaiser put it in 1946:[130] "he would be on the side of the progressive forces of the people today." Moreover, the large amount of decentralization (including the dissolution of Prussia into her provinces)[131] and the federalistic structure which Goerdeler favored, are far from being "anachronistic."

And there were other elements in his plans which cannot so easily be brushed aside. They breathe a certain soberness, a concrete—one may perhaps say an "Anglo-Saxon"—sense of "first things first," that is a realization of the necessity to rebuild a thoroughly disrupted community from the ground up; to take care of the basic content of political life and its competent administration, rather than of the showy side of party politics and emotional display. Under the conditions of a defeated and partially disintegrated Germany, the revival of those conventional features of a centralistic democratic machinery which had been introduced in Germany in 1919, could only amount to fiction anyway. Moreover, Goerdeler and his associates knew that no simple return to Weimar was possible. They wanted to

[129] Stein's influence upon Hassell is also evident (*op. cit.*, p. 77). The author may refer in this connection to his essay: "Stein und die Neugründung der Selbstverwaltung," in *Deutsche Beiträge* (Chicago, 1947), pp. 154-67.

[130] Ritter, *op. cit.*, p. 10.

[131] Pechel, *op. cit.*, p. 320. Popitz' draft of a preliminary constitutional law provided for the same dissolution as the "completion of Prussia's mission" (*Vom anderen Deutschland*, p. 387). Regarding the amount of decentralization, however, differences seem to have existed between Goerdeler's more liberal views and those of Popitz and Hassell.

avoid the loopholes in the parliamentary structure which had helped to make dictatorship possible: shifting governments and multiplicity of parties. And they warned against the corrupting system of elections by lists and the proportional distribution of seats. These warnings were certainly not out of date. They wanted also to avoid the specifically modern danger of irresponsible mass-propaganda and demagoguery which had been a source of deterioration under a formally perfect democratic regime.

Whether the means recommended—for example, the mixture of direct and indirect representation and the emphasis on occupational units—fitted the purpose and had any chance of satisfying genuine democratic needs, can of course be questioned. This was just one set of proposals, which merely indicates the general direction of thought. Discussion with a consultative body, the *Reichsrat*, was provided for, and might have led to considerable changes. It is clear, however, that within the "organic structure" of which Goerdeler spoke in one of his drafts,[132] the trade unions were supposed to play a major part—and, if their merger succeeded, were likely to play a decisive part. It cannot be proven, but it is quite possible that this is the point toward which Goerdeler's plans and those of Leuschner and J. Kaiser converged. It was a traditional trade-union policy to place practical achievements and step-by-step progress above party doctrine, demagogic agitation, and short cuts to the millennium. In this respect there seemed to be a common stock of ideas and a fair chance for political and social democracy to take root.

But a broader aspect must also be stressed. Goerdeler touched upon it by speaking of the "Democracy of the Ten Commandments."[133] Whatever his concrete constitutional plans, they had their center in those religious and humanist traditions and in those basic values which underlie the concepts of Western democracy. Thus, one of the many drafts of the radio address[134] which Goerdeler was to broad-

[132] Schlabrendorff, *op. cit.*, p. 84. This draft was formulated at the end of 1943.
[133] Pechel, *op. cit.*, p. 213.
[134] Schlabrendorff, *op. cit.*, pp. 83–90.

cast on becoming Chancellor, declared: "The German people must be allowed to pierce the fog of propaganda and learn the truth and nothing but the truth." The government, reads another sentence of the same document, "will establish a State sympathetic to Western Christian ideals, based upon the principles of civic duty, loyalty, self-sacrifice and efficient service for the commonwealth, as well as upon respect for the individual and his rights as a human being." It "initiates its work by subordinating the powers of the state to the laws of morality and justice." All religious communities were declared to be "free of State tutelage". Schools had to be cleared from the "pernicious part they were forced to play in falsifying facts, in offending against the adolescent instinct for Truth, in teaching phrases in place of knowledge, hypocrisy instead of courage, brutality instead of high endeavor. . . . Gifted children from all strata of the people, are to be admitted to all schools according to their abilities."

The same attitude of "regard for truth" and "veneration for justice" permeates all the documents which have become known.[135] In an appeal to the German people which Colonel General Beck was to issue, all stress was laid upon the moral degradation to which the previous regime had led, upon the blasphemous race theory, the hideous crimes, the soiling of German honor and decency. No easy promises were made. We shall have to struggle hard but we shall do so as "free men" and thus regain "tranquillity of conscience". The foremost task, another version of the radio address insisted, was the restoration of "the majesty of law." Persecution of Jews, crimes in occupied territories had to be expiated; and once more, in a final appeal, the task was described as one "of washing off the stains. . . . We Germans alone can and shall do that."

To borrow a current phrase, one may say that this was a program of "re-education"—a self-imposed one which called for a change of

[135] In addition to Schlabrendorff, Pechel prints in the Appendix an appeal to the army, to be signed by Von Witzleben, one to the German people, to be signed by Beck, one to the press, to be signed by Goerdeler, and another version of the radio address. According to Pechel, these documents were found by the Gestapo, a fact that is confirmed by the "SS Bericht."

mind, for repentance, and for a better way of life; for the return to Christian and humanist traditions, rather than for external requirements and formalized patterns of behavior. This re-education was meant to eradicate the Nazi slave-morale, not to implant a new one by indoctrination and censorship. It implied a task which could only be approached with a sense of humility rather than of self-righteousness, with a troubled conscience, and an awareness of the fact that all men are sinners.

In the same connection, it may be of interest to ask what the members of the shadow government thought about another current problem, for which the term "denazification" has become familiar. In one of their appeals they planned to say:[136] "The sword of justice must mercilessly strike those who reduced our fatherland to a caricature of a state, who banished decency and law, permitted and insisted upon corruption, and enriched themselves while the common people suffered poverty. . . . Furthermore, the responsibility of all those must be determined who in leading positions accepted and executed orders, without challenge, which they knew ran counter to law, conscience, and fact. Those too must be called to account who outside Germany violated international law and the honor and dignity of every decent human being. . . ."

It can be argued that this was not a complete list of crimes, and that it omitted to mention some subtler forms of the poison which had been spread through the period of ten years. Again it was Goerdeler's belief that there was only one front that mattered—that between the decent people and the "others"—and that there were no external labels upon which to base such a distinction.[137] Mere membership in a Nazi organization, therefore, did not constitute a crime. Anonymous denunciations were to be ignored, false ones were punishable, but everybody was called upon to advise the Minister of Justice of actual misdeeds, sins of omission as well as commission. There

[136] This version (and the translation) is taken from a manuscript of Mr. Lochner's.

[137] See Goerdeler's planned appeal to the press (Pechel, *op. cit.*, p. 311).

was to be no hesitancy regarding the real culprits, but there was little inclination to cast out the mere followers. And there was full awareness of the danger that in combating poison one may get poisoned oneself and end by adopting Hitlerite methods. If restoration of the majesty of law was a main purpose, it would simply not do to introduce laws *ex post facto*. It seemed un-Christian to appeal to vengeance, for whatever shoddy motives. And it seemed contrary to all established standards of lawful procedure to assume a defendant guilty until he proved his innocence. It was up to the prosecutor, rather, to prove his case. As far as one can judge on the basis of proclamations, the shadow government was determined thus to maintain one of the strongest elements of the Western heritage.

Turning to economic and social aspects,[138] it appears that Goerdeler was, in a specific sense, more "western" than most of his friends within the older generation. He was a firm believer in free competition. Economic life should be disturbed as little as possible by the state, and all red tape avoided. He therefore envisaged restoration of economic liberty and free trade, nationally and internationally—all this to a degree compatible with the common good. While stressing the right of property, he touched, as far as these programs show, neither the problem of large estates nor that of industrial concerns and monopolies. Only those employers were to be eliminated "who have debased their responsibility and become automatic receivers of orders from political bosses."

It was clearly over these views that the younger generation (that is, the men of the Kreisau circle) clashed with Goerdeler,[139] whereas Popitz and Hassell, who favored a planned economy and some sort of state socialism, were working as mediators. These differences, probably, and also Goerdeler's preference for parliamentary methods, caused Hassell to call him a "reactionary."[140] But it makes little sense

[138] See Schlabrendorff, *op. cit.*, pp. 88-89; Pechel, *op. cit.*, pp. 321-22.
[139] Hassell, *Diaries*, pp. 218-21; *Vom anderen Deutschland*, pp. 379-80 (the important document is left out in the American version).
[140] *Diaries*, pp. 214, 283, 333.

for American authors to repeat this reproach, unless one wants to call everything Western reactionary. Nor should Goerdeler's economic liberalism and his preference for free trade lead to the assumption that he was a social reactionary in any unqualified sense of the word, or an advocate of unfettered capitalism. In his municipal practice he had closely co-operated with the trade unions. A memorandum which he wrote in prison outlined the task of making the workers "partners in political responsibility."[141] In the economic sections of his program,[142] he spoke of a "creative participation" of employees in management and of the restoration of justice based on economic self-government. The development of wages, he declared, "is to be as far as possible subject to free wage agreements between employers and trade unions in which experienced mediation can offer helpful assistance." And he recommended the transfer of "the once admirable German Social Insurance system" (which after its introduction by Bismarck had become largely bureaucratic) to an "autonomous administration by the workers and employees."

While paying tribute to the sincerity of such intentions, one cannot and should not deny that here dividing lines appear. And it is no incidental fact that the term "restoration" occurs so often in Goerdeler's programs. Restoration of the majesty of law and of decent conduct, restoration of basic human values, of the dignity of man, of freedom of thought and creed—all these were primary demands. They rested with convictions which were steeled in fire; they were common to "right" and "left," and made these very terms meaningless. But the "blitz revolution" from above wanted also to restore order as quickly as possible and to prevent a real upheaval, involving not only such things as "lynch justice" but also a social revolution (another "November"). That the occupying powers of the West were likely to have the same aim does not matter in this hypothetical discussion. The critical point rather seems to be the program of economic liberty and the potential "restoration" of a society with pre-

141 Ritter, *op. cit.*, p. 10.
142 Pechel, *op. cit.*, p. 321; Schlabrendorff, *op. cit.*, pp. 88-89.

dominantly middle-class features. Was there still a basis for that, and if so, was it not rapidly shrinking? The trade unions which had found their place within a bourgeois world might concur in such a restoration. Would and could the socialists do likewise? And how were the masses, radicalized by oppression, impoverished, uprooted by bombing, evacuation, etc., to be fitted into such an order?

It can be argued and, in fact, has been argued that the overthrow of the Nazis was only the first step, that a "second revolution" would follow upon the revolution of the elite. This is, of course, entirely possible, though a matter of speculation. But to suppose that the socialist members of the conspiracy co-operated with such a reservation in mind, and looked forward toward Trojan horse tactics, seems to add false colors to the picture. In his last letter to his son, Leuschner wrote:[143] "Keep united, build up again." He may have had in mind only the trade-union front. But whoever tries to understand the spiritual climate of the opposition to Hitler will find in these words a broader meaning. It was not only that the barriers between churches and trade unions had been laid low. It also appears that, under the severest pressure, there had grown up among the representatives of opposite parties and classes—not harmony, exactly, but a fundamental trust and a comradeship of good will, which should not be obscured by party slogans, neither those of preceding nor of succeeding days.

This view is borne out in a specific sense, if we turn to the Kreisau circle, which united the strongest conservative, Christian and socialist elements, while adding the revolutionary, or at least "radical," impulse of a younger generation.

[143] Dulles, *op. cit.*, p. 105. See also W. v. Eckardt in *Neue Volkszeitung*, April 20, 1944.

6

The Kreisau Circle

Since the summer of 1940, a group of younger men, mostly men between thirty and forty years of age, had drawn together, forming a circle which centered around Count Helmuth James von Moltke, the great-grand-nephew of the Field Marshal of the Bismarckian era and grandson of a Chief Justice of Transvaal.[144] Before the war, he had practiced as a lawyer in Berlin. An uncompromising anti-Nazi, he arranged through his British friends to be admitted to the English bar. During the war he served with the High Command and the Intelligence Service as an adviser on international law. This position enabled him to protect a number of "people in danger" (as others likewise did) and to provide for legal arguments, and thereby to strengthen the resistance, against some of the most outrageous aspects of Hitlerian warfare.

The group of which he became the central figure took its name from the Moltke estate at Kreisau in Silesia.[145] Among the members were other aristocrats and bearers of old Prussian names. Next to Moltke, there stood Count Peter Yorck von Wartenburg, who has already been mentioned as a cousin of Stauffenberg. He had sprung from a family which included figures equally notable in military and political as well as in intellectual history. One of his ancestors was the general who by his "disobedience" in 1812 opened the war of liberation,[146] and another became known through the letters which

---

[144] For biographical details, see: *A German of the Resistance* (London, 1947), pp. 7-26.

[145] A general description of the circle and a brief characterization of the members has been given by the widows of the two leading figures (Marion Yorck and Freya Moltke; Kreisau, October 15, 1945). Pechel (*op. cit.*, pp. 116-19) followed this document closely. Some additional information (though not free of misunderstanding and error) is in Mr. Dulles' chapter.

[146] It is reported that the original of the famous "Convention of Tauroggen" is one of the few family possessions which has been saved from the Yorck estate.

he exchanged with his friend, the philosopher Dilthey. To the same aristocratic sector of the group there belonged Von Einsiedel and Von Trotha, a cousin of Moltke.

The participation of young East-Elbian noblemen in a radical circle (if "radical" means going down to the roots) is not as surprising as it may perhaps appear. Members of this group had had their share in the German youth movement of the twenties, whose main purpose was the revival of simplicity of life, purity of morals, and a sense of social responsibility contrasting with the outworn standards of a formalized society. Some of them were eager participants in the voluntary labor camps which brought young people of all classes together in an interchange of ideas and interests. It was with such experiences (the value of which cannot be invalidated by the Nazi distortion of these forms of "common life") and with strong religious convictions that they grew into manhood. To them, the inheritance of great estates implied responsibility rather than privilege. They considered in a sober and detached way the urgency of land reform, though they certainly would reject any "agrarian vandalism." In addition, there were specific insights and impulses which could be won in the eastern provinces of post-Versailles Germany, and which came to life at universities such as Breslau and Königsberg. The views which were discussed there, in classrooms, seminars, and debating clubs, referred to a frontier zone, with German and non-German peoples interlocked and intermingled to a degree which made the Western concept of the sovereign nation-state and the whole nineteenth-century idea of political nationality a reactionary scheme. Much serious thought was given, in these circles, to supranational and federalist solutions, to a disassociation of nationality from politics, to be effected in the form of cultural self-government (autonomy) and to international ethical standards, mutually binding for minorities on both sides of the frontier. The whole trend of these efforts centered upon peace between peoples as the only sound basis for peace between states, and ultimately upon the acceptance of a divine order which was to secure the dignity of the individual and of the family—of each profession, manual or intellectual, and of each national community—as the main-springs of a reformed society.

Again it is not surprising, therefore, that with men of such principled views, radical socialists like Mierendorff, Haubach, and Reichwein could intimately co-operate. All three were active members of the Kreisau circle. After Mierendorff's death Leber took his place. The religious element which linked these two wings together was specifically represented by four members of the group. On the one hand, by the Jesuit Delp, pastor in a Munich suburb, very influential among the Catholic youth (Cf p. 10), and by the provincial head of the Jesuits in Bavaria, Roesch—one of the older men of the group, whose balanced and mature opinion was of special value. On the other hand, two members of the Protestant Confessing Church were active within the circle: Harold Pölchau, the prison chaplain in Tegel (Cf. p. 10), and Eugen Gerstenmaier, a member of the External Affairs Office of the German Protestant Church, who is today, after a narrow escape, head of the Protestant Relief Society in Germany. He had long been convinced that "a spiritual opposition to Nazism was not enough, and that Nazism had to be rooted out if Christianity was to survive in Germany."[147] During the war, he was charged with the spiritual care of foreign workers. This activity, together with his participation in the Protestant ecumenical movement, gave him opportunities to travel abroad. His religious intensity and his broad philosophical outlook made him a particularly valuable member of the circle.

In addition, there were others who contributed particular experiences and their competence in special fields. Paulus van Husen, a Catholic from Westphalia, who had served on the mixed commission in Upper Silesia and as Counsellor of the Supreme Administrative Court; Hans Lukaschek, a Catholic lawyer, formerly *Oberpräsident* of Silesia; and Theodor Steltzer, who, after his removal from office as *Landrat* in Holstein, was active, like Gerstenmaier, in the ecumenical movement. During the war, he gave valuable support to the Norwe-

[147] Dulles, *op. cit.*, p. 116.

gian Underground; in fact, he saved the life of Bishop Berggrav, among others, and they in turn found a way to intervene in Steltzer's behalf and to prevent his execution in 1945.[148] The jurist Hans Peters of the University of Breslau also belonged to the Kreisau circle; like Steltzer and Reichwein, he was particularly active in adult education. Finally there were links with the oppositional group in the Foreign Office, through Johannes von Haeften and Adam Trott zu Solz. To the latter, this study will return in connection with his diplomatic actions. He was one of the most brilliant and dynamic members of the circle. Von Haeften was the son of a highly cultivated officer of the General Staff, who had become known in World War I because of his conflict with Ludendorff. Johannes, like his brother Werner (an aide-de-camp of Stauffenberg) was a devout Protestant. In the Kreisau documents he is praised for firmness of character and sensitiveness of conscience. Affiliated with Moltke and his friends were the younger Count von der Schulenburg (not to be confused with the former Ambassador), and Von Schwerin-Schwanenfeld, both of whom formed additional links with the military sector.

These were the men who gathered in small groups, whenever opportunity arose, and tried to outline certain programmatic views. There were, in particular, three meetings at Kreisau, in which the whole circle participated. Each meeting extended over several days —one in the spring of 1942, a second in the autumn of that year, and the third in the following spring. How Moltke himself interpreted the situation at about this time can be seen from a letter he was able to write in 1942, in the midst of war, to an English friend.[149] He spoke of the constant danger in which they lived and of the loosening of "the beast in man." But he also spoke of symptoms of hope: "the most important is the spiritual awakening, which is starting up, coupled as it is with the preparedness to be killed, if need be." While Moltke and his friends are themselves witnesses of a revivalist movement, he confirms the view (which has been expressed in this study)

[148] Details, *ibid.*, p. 91.
[149] *A German of the Resistance*, pp. 26-29.

that a regeneration of the spirit and a return to basic values was under way among groups of the German people who had gone through the testing furnace. Moltke found not only the churches increasing in strength, but the young generation caught by a new spirit. Today, he wrote, "it is beginning to dawn on a not too numerous but active part of the population, not that they have been misled, not that they are in for a hard time, not that they might lose the war, but that what is done is sinful and that they are personally responsible for every savage act that has been done, not, of course, in a mortal way, but as Christians."

In view of this situation Moltke and his friends saw it as their task to "visualize Europe after the war." "We can only expect," the letter continues, "to get our people to overthrow this reign of terror and horror if we are able to show a picture beyond the terrifying and hopeless immediate future. . . . For us Europe after the war is less a problem of frontiers and soldiers, of top-heavy organizations or grand plans, but Europe after the war is a question of how the picture of man can be re-established in the breasts of our fellow-citizens. This is a question of religion and education, of ties to work and family, of the proper relation of responsibility and rights." He added, that in their endeavor they felt greatly strengthened by contacts with "Christian groups in the various occupied territories with the exception of France, where, as far as we can find out, there is no really effective opposition on a fundamental basis, but only on the basis of casual activity."[150]

This attitude, this concern about a "fundamental basis," has been likened to a Gandhian "non-resistance."[151] Indeed similarities can be found, but such a statement nevertheless needs qualification. It

[150] While recognizing the splendid spirit of other people, Moltke remarked that "their position is easier than ours: moral and natural duties are congruous even to the simple-minded, while with us there is an apparent clash of duties." To the special case of the anti-Soviet Russian Resistance, which is somewhat similar to the German case, reference will be made later on.

[151] Gisevius, who has of course very little on the Kreisau circle, speaks of Moltke as an "advocate of inaction" (*op. cit.*, p. 435).

may be noted here, that Moltke spoke of getting "our people to over-throw this reign" by giving them a picture worth striving for. But it is true that the primary purpose of the Kreisau circle was not con-spiratorial activity and preparation for a plot. They wanted to lay the groundwork, rather, for a post-Nazi Germany and a post-Nazi Europe. No putsch, of course, could in itself heal the deep-seated evil. Moltke was inclined to think that it had to run its full course and that an internal revolt would only obscure the issue. It seems that he kept a certain distance from the activists. It is, therefore, to the thought of the Kreisau circle that we must first turn.

The leading ideas agreed upon among the members were set forth in a number of documents, of which five have been preserved.[152] They are dated May, 1942, and October, 1943. Again, as in the case of Goerdeler, these are not definite programs; later versions have been lost, and additional modifications were provided for. But the principles stand out very clearly. One is that the reconstruction had to be based on "freedom-loving labor" (*freiheitlich gesonnene Arbeiter-schaft*) and on the Christian churches. It would be a grave mistake to assume that this was a tactical compromise, a concession to the so-cialists in order to win them over for the acceptance of religious prin-ciples. All were firmly convinced that the totalitarian claim of the state could only be overcome by another, an other-worldly totalitar-ianism; that is, by a submission to ultimate and all-inclusive demands. Peter Yorck brought out this antithesis with supreme courage and logical precision when he declared in his trial before the People's Court: "The decisive factor . . . is the totalitarian claim of the state on the individual which forces him to renounce his moral and religious obligations to God."[153] And the presiding judge in Moltke's trial indirectly acknowledged this central theme of the Kreisau circle when

[152] The manuscripts are entitled: I. First Instruction for the special Commis-sioners (*Landesverweser*). II. Principles of Reconstruction. III. Result of Conferences regarding church and school matters. IV and V deal with "Dese-crators of the law."

[153] Dulles, *op. cit.*, p. 84. The statement of the presiding judge is in *A German of the Resistance*, p. 47.

he said: "Only in one respect does National Socialism resemble Christianity: we demand the whole man."

In this connection it is interesting to note that Moltke revealed a certain development in his views. Before the war (he said in the letter previously quoted) he had maintained that belief in God was not essential for an anti-Nazi stand. He now thought that he had been "wrong, completely wrong," and that right ethical principles were not sufficient to make people ready for risking and sacrificing everything.

Whatever the validity of such a statement, Tresckow or Lehndorff, Goerdeler or Hermann Kaiser, Hammerstein or Von Kleist could have said the same, as would have many thousands of unknown people. And the radical labor leaders did not differ. Experience must have brought them very close to the source of strength which was apparent among conservative radicals. And they must have left behind some of the blinkers of Marxist orthodoxy. Otherwise it would be unthinkable that the outlines, jointly arrived at, placed a thorough emphasis on God's order as the yardstick for regulating social and international relations and as the only binding force that could overcome arbitrary power and an unbridled technocracy. In fundamental matters, absolute freedom of conscience, protection of family life, and social co-operation were consequences of this view. The schools maintained by the state were to be "Christian" schools, with religious instruction obligatory and given by representatives of the churches.[154]

It would lead too far afield to discuss other educational ideas of the Kreisau circle, though they are not uninteresting in view of to-day's controversies. They demanded new textbooks and the withdrawal of the old ones even before the new were ready. At the same time they were very much opposed to mere pragmatism and "behav-

[154] This has been misunderstood by Dulles, who assumes that elementary education was "to be largely in the hands of the churches" (*op. cit.*, p. 95). Dulles also seems to think of the Kreisau circle too much in terms of a tactical compromise (*ibid.*, p. 93).

118

iorism." They insisted on preserving the classical tradition of the German high school, and on separating professional schools from universities, the latter to be devoted to the old "universal" studies only. The relationship between the state and the churches was to be regulated on the basis of free contracts. For the future, a "German Christianity" was hoped for, to which all Christians should adhere, regardless of dogma.

More specifically, Christian ethics and the "dignity of man" were to underlie the economic system, and here the progressive element of thought emerges distinctly. An "ordered system of competition" is demanded, including a large amount of economic self-government. This system implied dissolution of monopolistic cartels and concerns, agrarian reforms, the nationalization of key industries, factory communities with participation of the employees in management and in surplus dividends. It also implied the "one" German trade union, of which Goerdeler and Leuschner spoke. It seems, however, that the Kreisau circle assigned to this organ a transitional task only, until the restoration of an ordered economic life could be left to the state on the one hand, or self-governing chambers of industry, commerce, handicraft, and agriculture on the other. Throughout, the principle was stressed that the natural resources should serve the common good and the influence and responsibility of the German workers be increased.

While the strong admixture of socialist elements characterizes the economic planning of the Kreisau circle as one "between East and West," and puts it practically next to British Labor policies of today, their legal concepts were thoroughly Western. In fact, the two drafts which deal with the punishment of "desecrators of law," the divine and natural as well as the statutory law, belong to the finest expressions of the *Rechtsstaat* idea. The proposals went considerably farther than those proclaimed by Goerdeler; they included a procedure before the Hague court in certain cases, and they had obviously benefited from Moltke's juristic training and his experiences as an international lawyer, as well as from the strict moralism of the Kreisau circle. But the insistence upon the "majesty of the law" did not differ from Goerdeler's attitude. Moltke, therefore, very carefully discussed the problem of "retroactive legislation" and the principle of "*nulla poena sine lege*" (no punishment without law). He appraised this principle historically as a barrier against absolutistic arbitrariness, and though he declared it not to be valid generally and everywhere, he found it so fundamental to civilized concepts that under no conditions should it be set aside. The solution of the dilemma which he suggested provided for the apprehending of all sufficiently suspect (to whom the old German principle of the "ban" might be applied) and for the competence of the ordinary penal courts to issue "declaratory" statements. To be thus declared a "desecrator of law" (*Rechtsschänder*) would imply a certain atonement, and such a declaration would at the same time satisfy, or reawaken, the sense of justice, establish a precedent for future procedures, and act as a deterrent to perversion of law. It might be followed up by administrative measures curtailing civil or political rights. While Moltke thus wanted to avoid the danger of lawless vindictiveness and arbitrariness, he held that most of the Nazi crimes (including complicity and obedience to orders of a criminal nature) fell under existing law anyhow, and could be tried in a normal way.

Regarding international crimes the proposals are no less interesting. Moltke stressed as strictly as possible the necessity of a lawfully ordered comity of nations. Just because of this ideal, however, he thought an ethical solution must be found, one which could not be interpreted as vengeance of the victors but which represented clearly the "triumph of law." A fiction of justice was, in his view, bound to have a destructive effect. Moltke therefore suggested giving to the Court of International Justice at the Hague the same competence to issue declaratory statements regarding desecrators of law which he wanted to give to German courts. In cases dealing with crimes which could be tried under positive law—either international law or the law of the countries concerned—he suggested that the court be composed of six judges, three from the victor nations, two from the neutral states, and one from the defeated nation. Prosecution was to lie with the nation whose laws had been violated; execution of the verdict, however, with any other than the plaintiff nation. Once more he added the warning that progress in international morality could result only from acknowledging the supremacy of law, not from answering force with force. Regarding the extent of persecution, he recalled the English experience of 1689 as described by Macaulay: ". . . the ringleaders, the men of rank, fortune and education, whose power and artifices have led the multitude into error, are the proper objects of severity. The deluded population, when once the slaughter on the field of battle is over, can scarcely be treated too leniently."

Two other drafts of the Kreisau circle dealt with the political reorganization of Germany. While in the letter to his English friend of 1942, Moltke acknowledged that their fight might end with Germany's "total collapse as a national unit," the practical proposals were made in the hope of being able to rebuild a federative whole first in Germany and then in Europe. Instructions were set up for special commissioners (*Landesverweser*) who, after the overthrow or the collapse of the regime, should take charge of the provinces. These were to be established instead of the old historic states, each with populations of three to five millions and with boundaries approximately following those of the military districts. The first tasks of the commissioners were to secure the supply of food, to purge the political personnel and to begin, in co-operation with the trade unions and the churches, the restoration of law and decency as well as the reform of the administrative and economic system.

The long-range program of reconstruction was set forth in a lengthy document. It stressed those religious and social concepts which have already been discussed. More specifically, it outlined a structure of the German Reich which was to be in harmony with the natural articulation of human life in family, local community, and district. Political responsibility should develop within the smaller cells, that is, within concrete units of neighborhood, and within a framework of problems with which the common man was familiar. Hence, the representatives of the local community and of the district (*Kreis*) only were to be directly elected.[155] Suffrage was to be granted to every citizen over twenty-one, with the head of the household having an additional vote for each child under this age. Representatives had to be at least twenty-seven years old. "Bearers of arms" were not eligible.[156] The primary assemblies of town and district would then elect the representatives of the provinces, and these in turn would elect the Reichstag. Provisions were to be made to the effect that in both cases at least half the number of the elected was not taken from the electing bodies. The provincial diets and the Reichstag were to elect the provincial Commissioner (*Landeshauptmann*) and the Reichspresident respectively. Both were to serve for twelve years. The chancellor, who forms his own cabinet, is to be appointed by the president with the consent of the Reichstag. A qualified majority of parliament can enforce his dismissal. In addition there was to be a Central Council (*Reichsrat*) composed of the provincial commissioners, the president of the Reichstag,[157] the chiefs of the economic councils and appointees. This upper chamber was to be a consultative body, but also to be invested with jurisdiction over the Reichsgovernment and the provincial governments.

It has seemed necessary to render these proposals in some detail, because only so can a basis be reached for a real understanding of the contrast between the older and younger generations. In fact, we have definite evidence that they clashed. The most striking is a letter by Dr. Gerstenmaier[158] which describes a meeting in December,

[155] Dulles errs in assuming that local officials (!) and the provincial diets were to be elected by the people (*ibid.*, p. 94).

[156] This author could not find any evidence which bears out Mr. Dulles' statement that in the view of the Kreisau circle "the German army was to be abolished" (*ibid.*, p. 95). On the contrary (and quite naturally) the existence of "bearers of arms" (probably, in the main, a national militia) was presupposed, as it is in any known democracy.

[157] Dulles (*loc. cit.*) confuses this with the President of the Reich.

[158] *Vom anderen Deutschland*, pp. 379-80 (omitted in the American version of Hassell's diaries). The Diaries (p. 283) show that the conference actually took place late in January, 1943. They give a very accurate summary. Some further hints about the problem of the two generations can be found on pp. 318, 321, 327.

1942, or January, 1943. He states expressly that the discussion had been prepared for weeks and presented "one of the most interesting events in the preparation for the coup d'état." And he also states that the difference was not exactly that between young and old, but between the younger people and Goerdeler, and that its fundamental character was brought to the fore in social and economic matters. Participants were Beck, Goerdeler, Popitz, Hassell, Jessen, and the nucleus of the Kreisau circle. Beck, we are told, was merely listening, while Popitz and Hassell were mediating. Moltke became very polemical, and eventually it fell to Gerstenmaier, in the absence of Haubach and Mierendorff, to formulate the economic and social views of the Kreisau circle in "sharp antithesis" to those of Goerdeler.

This evidence, which has been overlooked in most discussions, corroborates what likewise can be derived from a comparison of the respective programs. Fundamentally, the Kreisau circle (like so many neoconservatives or members of the youth movement in the twenties) had broken with the bourgeois mentality, with most of the tenets of nineteenth-century liberalism, as well as with the social and economic concepts of Weimar. In this they were more distant from Goerdeler than from the others. But the Christian convictions which they held in common formed a strong link, and Goerdeler, as former mayor of Königsberg, was not unfamiliar with the trends of thought which had spread among young people in the East. For him, no less than for Moltke, the statement was valid that re-establishment of the dignity of man was "a question of religion and education, of ties to work and family, of the proper relation of responsibility and rights." In fact, if one goes into the details of comparison there appears a large area of common ground, particularly as far as Goerdeler's insistence on the influence and responsibility of the working class is concerned. It is quite possible that in the years between 1942 and 1944 the Kreisau circle exerted an influence in this direction, and had already begun to permeate Goerdeler's world.

Less distinct are the political differences. The Kreisau circle, including its socialist members, adhered no more than did Goerdeler to a formal democratic setup and to the French theory of the nation one and indivisible, or of popular sovereignty. Both sides, rather, were concerned about "democracy of the grass-roots," about building from the ground up. In fact, Goerdeler went farther in applying the principle of direct democratic elections, but not quite as far in the matter of decentralization; and his constitutional program seems to have been on the whole less clear-cut. But it shows no tendency contradictory to, or exclusive of, the political ideas which were alive in the Kreisau circle. We are told[159] that Leber, the leading Socialist, did not find Goerdeler's program "constructive enough" but believed that, as Minister of the Interior in Goerdeler's cabinet, he would be able to achieve his aims. And Haubach, as Minister of Information, would have had a good chance to disseminate Kreisau ideas.

From all this the conclusion may safely be drawn that the contrast between the older and the younger generation within the German opposition, or that between restorative and revolutionary tendencies, should not be overstressed[160] and that there is little ground to speculate about the necessity of a rupture. On the contrary, it appears that the amount of agreement was surprisingly large. The Kreisau circle aimed at restoration too, at the re-establishment of the picture of man "in the breasts of our fellow citizens." In this re-education they saw a primary prerequisite of democracy. That was not so far from Goerdeler's "Democracy of the Ten Commandments." Like Goerdeler too, they provided for conservative checks; for example, regarding the age of those eligible, or the influence of an irresponsible popular will such as had helped to pave the way for Hitler. Their revolutionary impulse did not center upon the blue print ("grand plans") of a new society; it was radical in its demand to abandon a materialistic past and to revive those moral forces in which Goer-

[159] By Marion Yorck and Freya Moltke in their memorandum (see p. 112, n. 145).

[160] In this respect the author differs from the views of Salin (see p. 78, n. 66), who heavily emphasizes the difference between the older (restorative) and the younger (revolutionary) generation. The same distinction, in much cruder and more tendentious form, in: *Neue Auslese* (see p. 21, n. 23).

deler likewise believed. Their specific contribution to the resistance was a leaven working from within rather than from without, and a stock of ideas, refreshing, but not incompatible with, those of the older generation.

There was, however, another difference from Goerdeler and his group, upon which Countess von Moltke has laid stress. According to one of her statements "her husband and his more radical friends never approved of Goerdeler's active plans and would have nothing to do with his hazardous conspiracy."[161] This "Ghandian" element has already been touched upon but needs some clarification because of the basic character of the problem involved. Again there exists the danger of misinterpreting a very essential feature of the German opposition. Practically none of the major conspirators had been entirely spared the searching question, whether violence was permitted or could be a remedy at all. None was of the adventurous or a-social type of "resister." And yet they answered in the affirmative with the strongest motive being that expressed by Tresckow, a motive of a categoric character: "We must prove to the world and to future generations that the men of the German Resistance movement dared to take the decisive step and to hazard their lives upon it." It can be proved that, of the Kreisau group, Gerstenmaier shared this view from the angle of religious responsibility. Spiritual resistance was not enough. And in addition, Gerstenmaier's letter[162] furnishes explicit evidence. It characterizes the meeting of the older and the younger generation in January, 1943, as "one of the most interesting events in the preparation of the coup d'état," and it ends with the statement that all participants (that is, including Moltke) agreed upon the necessity "to arrange for the coup d'état as quickly as possible."

In fact, members of the circle took active part in the preparations (Yorck, for example), and Gerstenmaier was arrested by the Gestapo at the headquarters of the revolt on July 20, 1944. The assumption that Moltke, had he been at liberty, would have done everything in

[161] *Round Table*, June, 1946, p. 229 n.
[162] See p. 122, n. 158.

his power to prevent the attempt seems to be highly questionable.[163] The dividing line between thought and action which actually existed was much more delicate. As Countess von Moltke herself says in another of her statements, the Kreisau circle never excluded "the employment of force."[164] Their specific task, however, they saw in filling the spiritual and political vacuum which, in their opinion, would follow from the loss of the war and the collapse of the regime, whether it ran its course to the very end or was overthrown. That this difference came out so clearly was, in Moltke's own view, an event of God's, not of man's making.

This interpretation is borne out by two extraordinary documents, the two letters which Moltke wrote to his wife after the trial in January, 1945. In one of them he states almost jubilantly[165] that he was going to die precisely for what he had done; not for having plotted, but for having thought, for something "which is worthwhile." He paid tribute to the political acumen of Freisler, the dreaded and brutal president of the People's Court, who had set him apart from all practical activity and from the Goerdeler faction. Thus the letter concludes: "Our case-histories provide documentary proof that it is neither plots nor plans but the very spirit of man that is to be hunted down. Long live Freisler."

No historical comment can improve upon these final words. They may sink in with their full weight. But Moltke himself has added an

[163] This view is held by Salin (*op. cit.*, p. 726) and by the editor of the Moltke letters in *Round Table*, *op. cit.*, p. 221. Unfortunately his Preface extols Moltke so much at the expense of others that Moltke himself would have been the first to protest. Thus the Preface states that the other conspirators are "not unfairly" characterized by the watchword of the cartoonist: "Unless we get out of this war quickly, we shan't be ready to fight the next. . . . They were thinking along the traditional lines of Prussian militarism." It is a pity that these ignoble distortions occur in an article which has had the privilege of first printing some of the noblest human documents. Not much better is Gisevius' attempt at playing off the "balanced" and "moderate" Moltke (from whom he was certainly worlds apart) against the "dynamic" and "careless" Stauffenberg (*op. cit.*, p. 473).

[164] *Round Table*, June, 1946, p. 229 n.

[165] *Ibid.*, pp. 228-30.

interpretation. In the second letter[166] he praised God for having so wonderfully "moulded his unworthy vessel. . . . At the very moment when the danger became acute that I might be drawn into active preparation for an uprising (Stauffenberg came to see Peter [Yorck] on the evening of the 19th [July, 1944]), I was removed so that I was and still am innocent of all connection with the use of violence. . . ." Thus it was a higher dispensation which had "removed" him in January, 1944, in order to bring out the full meaning of his life. There was during the trial, he wrote, no talk of a "tortuous character," of "complicated thinking," or of "ideology." He also praised the guidance of God which had divorced him from all class interests and all patriotic motives, so that he could bear witness to the most fundamental force of resistance. "I stood before Freisler," he wrote in another final sentence, "not as a protestant, not as a great landowner, not as a noble, not as a Prussian, not as a German even. . . . No, I stood there as a Christian and nothing else."

Besides this profound interpretation of the part which the Kreisau circle and its foremost representative played in the events, there remains a minor and merely factual question. Did not the "advocates of inaction" indirectly put the conspiracy under pressure and thus precipitate the attempt? Moltke was arrested in January, 1944, because he had warned Otto C. Kiep who was wanted by the Gestapo. On June 22, Leber and Reichwein approached the Central Committee of the Communist Underground. This attempt to broaden the front had fateful consequences, as has been mentioned before. It brought the Gestapo, which had penetrated into the Communist ranks, onto the right track. A few days later Leber and Reichwein were arrested too. In view of these events it has been said that Stauffenberg simply had to act in order to rescue his friends and prevent the full disclosure of the plot.[167] If one remembers, however, that action had been continuously tried since February, 1943, and by Stauffenberg

[166] *A German of the Resistance*, pp. 47-49. This letter is not contained in the *Round Table* edition.
[167] Henk, *op. cit.*, p. 54.

himself since December, 1943, such a thesis does not seem to have much weight.

But the contact with the Communists raises a more important question. Does it prove an "Eastern" orientation of the Kreisau circle (and Stauffenberg) as against the "Western" orientation of Goerdeler and his associates? Was it, as Gisevius has tried to persuade us, the "militant socialism" of Leber, or Stauffenberg's "militaristic view" which led the group of younger men into the camp of a national bolshevism?[168] No graver misinterpretation could be offered, nor could the primary motive be more badly mistaken which Stauffenberg had in common with the men of Kreisau: the front against totalitarianism of whatever political or social color. Among the many disservices which the "crown witness" Gisevius has rendered to the understanding of important issues, his caricature of Stauffenberg is probably the worst. He depicts him as a "Super-Prussian," military to the core, whom only defeat shook into opposition and to whom salvation of the fatherland was equivalent to the salvation of the army. Along the same line, Gisevius reports (and had also told Mr. Dulles)[169] that Stauffenberg was hoping for a Communist Germany organized after the Russian model and supported by the Red Army. In contrast, it may be stated here in a preliminary way, that Stauffenberg, like the

[168] *Op. cit.*, pp. 485, 487, 503: "The young colonel could not and would not deny his origins in authoritarian National Socialism" [!] On the next page the reader is even told that Stauffenberg wanted a military dictatorship of "true National Socialists." In keeping with this kind of approach, Gisevius analyzes the "rude" and "boorish" colonel (the disciple of Stefan George!) as a "frustrated" man trying to "overcompensate for the inferiority feelings engendered by his mutilation." To anyone who reads Gisevius' memoirs with a modicum of historical criticism, it is obvious that the inferiority complex and the feelings of resentment are on his side. He felt clearly that the younger and more socialistically minded generation did not trust him. It may be mentioned that the "SS Bericht" also mistakes the Kreisau circle as "pinks", and Stauffenberg as attached to Soviet Russia.

[169] Dulles, *op. cit.*, p. 170. It is quite understandable that Gisevius, who gave so much valuable information to the American Intelligence Service, is given high credit by Mr. Dulles. In the use of memoirs as source material, however, the elementary rules of historical criticism, referred to in the previous note, cannot be set aside.

128

other men of Kreisau, had a universal rather than a militaristic or nationalistic outlook; that he thought in terms of liberation for all people who suffered under a tyrannical regime, certainly not in terms of replacing one such regime in Germany by another.[170]

A further discussion of the East-West issue must be left to the next chapter which has to deal with the German opposition as part of the great international struggle, with the efforts of Germans to prevent a total catastrophe in the center of Europe, and with the Allied attitude toward these endeavors.

[170] See Karl Michel, *Ost und West, Der Ruf Stauffenbergs* (1947). To this book, of course, the same criticism has to be applied. It is to a large extent fictitious, but in the description of Stauffenberg's antitotalitarianism (expressed long before Stalingrad and before his mutilation) and of his relation to the anti-Soviet volunteers of the East (the main subject matter of the book) there is contained much genuine and valuable information.

INTERNATIONAL ASPECTS

1

Peace Moves

THE German opposition to Hitler, though covered with silence and eventually with abuse, was an internationally well-known fact. And those in charge of Western diplomacy cannot claim to have been ignorant of pertinent details. They knew about the socialist and communist underground, of which the "Green Reports" and other "inside" sources gave a more or less specified picture. In addition, they were directly informed and entreated by a number of Germans who were active in the conspiracy, by men in private as well as in official positions, military or civilian. They were offered co-operation and concerted resistance at a time when it was still possible to forestall war and to put an end to the nightmare of a gangster regime, not only over Germany but over large parts of Europe.

It has been shown that Lord Halifax and other Englishmen were fully aware of the attitude and the plans of the German opposition in the summer and autumn of 1938. And it is not without a broader interest to examine the speeches and announcements by which Winston Churchill, immediately thereafter, answered Hitler's oratory. Broadcasting to the United States from London, on October 17,[1] Churchill replied to Hitler's accusation that if he or his friends were in power, their aim would be immediate war with Germany. On the contrary, said Churchill, if he himself, or Anthony Eden, or Duff Cooper had been Prime Minister, a league of collective security would have been formed, formidable enough to deter the German dictator from war. And he added: "This would have been an opportunity for all the peace-loving and moderate forces in Germany, together with the chiefs of the German army, to make a great effort to re-establish something like sane and civilized conditions in their own country."

[1] *Times* (London), October 17, 1938, p. 16, col. 2.

130

Thus Churchill not only knew about the existence and the concrete aims of the "peace-loving and moderate forces" and of the "chiefs of the German army"; he was even bold, we may say reckless, enough to give out by these words what had been very confidential information. Hitler, of course, was quick to pick up the allusion to a German opposition movement, and Churchill, in a release to the press[2] on November 7, found it necessary to soothe the wrath of the aroused dictator. "I have always said," he stated, "that if Great Britain were defeated in war, I hoped we should find a Hitler to lead us back to our rightful position among the nations. I am sorry, however, that he has not been mellowed by the great success that has attended him." This was not exactly a support of the German opposition, which blamed Hitler for more than lacking mellowness; but it was obviously meant to calm down the Führer's suspicious mood. Thus Churchill continued: "Herr Hitler showed himself unduly sensitive about suggestions that there may be other opinions in Germany besides his own. It would be indeed astonishing if, among 80,000,000 of people so varying in origin, creed, interest and condition, there should be only one pattern of thought. It would not be natural; it is incredible."

One cannot say that the Germans failed in efforts to corroborate the view, that there was not only "one pattern of thought." In December, 1938, Goerdeler sent to his friends abroad a program for world peace, in which he suggested a preliminary conference of all powers, aiming at financial stability, a binding international statute, and gradual disarmament.[3] "He who refuses to participate, wants war and is a breaker of peace." In the summer of 1939 Goerdeler, "with the approval of the generals,"[4] again visited England, America, and France. He approached numerous leading statesmen and acquainted them with the situation in Germany. Among them were

[2] *Ibid.*, November 7, 1938, p. 12, col. 2. For a qualification of this often quoted appraisal of Hitler, see p. 24, n. 3.

[3] Goerdeler's *Politisches Testament*, pp. 47-52.

[4] Hassell, *Diaries*, p. 221.

Churchill, Sumner Welles, Daladier, and Vansittart. "Yes, Vansittart," as the American historian, Harold C. Deutsch, adds with justifiable emphasis.[5] In fact, we are told that as late as February, 1940, Vansittart sent Goerdeler his regards "with the comment that now it would not be so easy to put through the old Reich frontiers in the East."[6] There were other efforts in the summer of 1939—those of Hassell and Schlabrendorff, and of Trott and Kordt, to which reference has been made.

But after the outbreak of war, diplomats and statesmen of the Western powers began to speak and act as if no opposition to Nazism existed or had ever become known to them. Although Neville Chamberlain, in his addresses, clearly concentrated on "the German Government"[7] as standing in the way of peace, he made no appeal to "another Germany" and in a letter of January, 1940, he said:[8] "I am afraid, that the Germans are very far from that frame of mind which will be necessary before they are prepared to listen to what we should call reason." While this may be called a defensible statement, in view of the propaganda effect which Hitler's withholding of truth, his method of opening the war on a fraudulent pretext, as well as his first victories, had in Germany, the Western statesmen soon went further. The identification of Nazis and Germans was accentuated, as the area of war was extended, and became one of the main lines of official propaganda.[9]

[5] In a review of Mr. Dulles' book which comments upon the obvious gaps in his presentation (*American Historical Review*, January, 1948, p. 338).

[6] That is what Goerdeler told Hassell (*Diaries*, p. 111). The "old frontiers" meant those of 1914. Goerdeler and Hassell certainly were hoping for that. In contrast, see Trott's program of the frontiers of 1933 as a minimum.

[7] An example is his speech in the House of Commons, October 12, 1939 (Hansard's *Parliamentary Debates*, Vol. 352, pp. 566-67).

[8] Keith Feiling, *Life of Neville Chamberlain* (1946), pp. 427-28.

[9] A notable exception was Dorothy Thompson's broadcasts ("Listen Hans") which were addressed to Helmuth von Moltke. It is a matter of fairness to add that the identification referred to did not include Germans outside Germany in any schematic way. The policy of summarily interning "enemy aliens" which was adopted in England in the grave situation after Dunkirk was soon revised under the pressure of British public opinion. In the United

In spite of this attitude, the German opposition certainly did not relax its efforts. Contacts were taken up through numerous channels. It is neither possible nor necessary to enumerate them all. Connections with the Vatican (and through the Vatican with Western countries) were carried on mainly by the Munich lawyer Joseph Müller, a member of the Intelligence Service and at the same time a diplomatic agent of Cardinal Faulhaber, the Archbishop of Munich. Early in 1940, Beck communicated with the former Centrist Chancellor Joseph Wirth, an exile in Switzerland, and asked him to make use of his Anglo-French contacts.[10] The opposition at that time wanted to secure a wait-and-see attitude on the part of the Western powers, in case the military putsch came off before Hitler attacked in the West. Other members of the Catholic opposition, and likewise of the Foreign Office, used Dr. Brüning as liaison.

Particularly active, of course, was Von Hassell, the former ambassador, who had many channels at his disposal. He met repeatedly with British emissaries in Switzerland, and also with Professor Karl Burckhardt, the former High Commissioner of the League in Danzig. Moreover, up to November, 1940, Hassell was in close contact with Alexander Kirk, the United States Chargé d'Affaires in Berlin, and

States only a modicum of security measures was imposed upon immigrants of German descent, and there was nothing comparable to the Germanophobia of World War I. This leads to a general remark which has some bearing upon this part of our study. To everybody who has lived through the two World Wars on whatever side of the fence, one difference, besides many others, must have been very impressive. It has been justly said that in July, 1914, all governments were more or less pacific, or at least afraid of a general war, whereas all nations were more or less bellicose and rose in enthusiasm. Nothing of such a popular emotion was in existence in 1939 on either side, but a grim determination rather. When the United States entered the war, this meant in popular estimate "a dirty job" which simply had to be done. There were none of those elemental outbursts of hatred which had occurred in 1917-18; "sauerkraut" and "dachshund" continued their peaceful existence, German music continued to be played, and a spirit of fairness and soberness prevailed within the general public. The same cannot be said of policy-making circles and of the official propaganda line, as far as it concerns the subject of this study.

[10] Dulles, op. cit., pp. 59-60 ("An ambiguous, non-committal answer arrived, just as the offensive in the West began").

with an American businessman ("Mr. Stallforth"). When, in February, 1940, Mr. Sumner Welles came to visit Berlin, Hassell urged Kirk to have the American Undersecretary of State "meet other than official personages."[11] This did not work out, except for an interview with Schacht. On the contrary, the visit of Sumner Welles, however differently it was meant, was a disappointment to the opposition, because it seemed to increase Hitler's prestige as a possible partner in peace negotiations. In vain, Goerdeler tried to suggest that the American diplomat should not go from Rome directly to Berlin, but first to Paris and London. "There he would be so enlightened that he would give up."

These are some mere glimpses of activities which were meant to inform and warn the Western statesmen as well as to explore possibilities of peace and the chances of a lasting settlement in case a new German government took over. In the same vein were Goerdeler's discussions with the King of the Belgians, who in March, 1940, "was ready to be of assistance, if a change in regime should occur.[12] And time and again, through three years, Goerdeler had the opportunity to talk with the bankers Wallenberg in Stockholm about the possibility of a coup d'état.[13] He explained to them the plans of the opposition, obviously with the desire of receiving an advance consent from the Allies. This, he was told by the Wallenbergs, was impossible, but on their suggestion he drew up, in May, 1943, a memorandum "regarding all the points which the new regime would accept, such as punishment of war criminals, war damages, disarmament, democratic regime, etc." What Goerdeler, in turn, requested was that "as soon as the coup occurred the Allies discontinue bombing German cities, in order to show the German people they were well disposed toward the new regime. Furthermore, he desired that as far as possible Berlin and Leipzig be spared during the next few days, as

[11] *Diaries*, p. 114. The following, *ibid.*, p. 112. On the visit, see Sumner Welles, *The Time for Decision*, pp. 91-120.

[12] Von Hassel, *Diaries*, p. 120.

[13] See the summarizing statement by J. Wallenberg (Dulles, *op. cit.*, pp. 142-46).

the central organizations of the anti-Nazi movement were located at these points and a disruption of communications would make a coup more difficult." All this was, of course, passed on to the British.

Other neutral points of contact were Spain, Portugal, and Turkey. Among the minor figures who co-operated with Hassell in using these channels may be mentioned Albrecht Haushofer,[14] the son of the geopolitician and author of the "Moabiter Sonnette" which he wrote in prison, and which belong to the most impressive spiritual documents of the German resistance.

While we know a good deal about the fact but little about the content of the various soundings, some of the diplomatic actions and peace moves stand out in clearer profile.

One of them centered around Adam von Trott zu Solz, who has been mentioned as an early anti-Nazi writer and a member of the Kreisau circle. He was a former Rhodes scholar, the son of a Prussian Minister of Education, the grandson of Von Schweinitz, who had been an ambassador in Bismarck's time, and of an American grandmother, who in turn was a great-grandchild of John Jay, the first Chief Justice of the Supreme Court. Thus Trott, like Moltke, had a partly Anglo-Saxon background; also, like Moltke, he was a link between the aristocratic and the socialistic groups of the opposition, a close friend of Leuschner and later of Leber. For some time he did research work in China, and then entered the Foreign Office to make use of this cover for his anti-Nazi activities.

Trott had been in London in summer, 1939.[15] Though his overtures regarding the German opposition and the moral support which it needed were "icily" received by Chamberlain, he had many English friends in official circles. And it was obviously on instruction of the British Foreign Office that he was able to reach the United States, via Gibraltar (!) in October, 1939. His ostensible purpose was

[14] A report of his brother, Dr. Heinz Haushofer, deals partly with peace soundings preceding the Twentieth of July. An English translation of the "Moabiter Sonette," by Ernst Feise, has been published in *Neue Rundschau*, January, 1946.

[15] This and the following on personal information.

to attend a Conference of the Institute for Pacific Relations in New York.[16] What he actually did during his three-months' stay was, as he told Felix Morley, then editor of the Washington Post,[17] to devote himself "to developing a receptive attitude here towards the big change which, he thinks, is coming in Germany. . . . The chief problem is how to insure that a war of extermination against the Nazis will not force behind them all the elements beginning to cohere for Hitler's overthrow."

There is no doubt that Trott had important conversations along these lines. He informed high officials of the Department of State and other policy makers about the aims and personalities of the Underground. Whether he was in a position to formulate definite "terms upon which the opposition hoped to terminate the war, after Hitler's overthrow," and to add "a pledge to prosecute the principal Nazi leaders for common crimes," cannot be fully ascertained.[18] The memorandum which he eventually turned in pointed in a different direction and had a more general scope. It advocated a timely clarification of war aims in order to "reassure and consolidate opposition in Germany and thereby contribute to the discrediting and undoing of Nazi domination."

To support this proposal Trott stressed the fact that the increasing dissatisfaction with, or indignation at, Hitler's rule was counteracted by "the dire necessity of the German people to back the regime in its war against the alleged intention of the Allied powers to destroy Germany. . . ." The task on hand, therefore, was to make clear that "continued National Socialist control is the chief obstacle to peaceful survival" and that by removal of the government "a tolerable po-

[16] Dulles (*op. cit.*, p. 89) has a few lines on that, but very little on the more important features of the episode.

[17] See excerpts from Felix Morley's diary (November 20, 1939) in the article by Alexander B. Maley, *Human Events*, February 27, 1946.

[18] According to Mr. Maley's article, this was the content of a secret memorandum which was also delivered to Lord Lothian, the British Ambassador. However, the memorandum from the draft of which the following quotations are taken, and which is used here for the first time, has a different content. There may have been several such drafts.

sition for Germany in a new Europe could be secured." If, however, no constructive line would be taken by the Western powers, there was, in Trott's view, the imminent danger of a national bolshevism which might not keep within the German borders. Thus far, he stated quite correctly, the war has been carried on without any "frenzy of passion." Frenchmen and Britishers are not fighting for "glory," "prestige" or "national grandeur," but defending their personal liberties and their way of life. To maintain this "rational and deliberate attitude," the permanence of which is threatened by increasing sacrifices, a "clear objective" is necessary, an objective, "the emotional as well as the rational appeal of which justifies the terrible sacrifices which are demanded. . . . It is imperative to tell the people, not only why they were forced to fight, but moreover what they are fighting for."

This general suggestion was supplemented by more concrete considerations. It should be possible for the Allied governments "to state certain maximum concessions which are going to be asked of the German people or to assure, that their territorial status of 1933 [that is, the Versailles status] shall be disputed under no circumstances." In addition, certain minimum commitments on the Allied side should be considered regarding economic concessions and general conditions, "which would enable Germany to participate in a cooperative European future." As to Germany's own contribution, it must consist not only in the overthrow of her present leadership; "there must be assurance also that the Germany emerging after the downfall of Hitler will be an honest and effective partner to peace." While pointing to a separate discussion of the changes required in Germany's social, economic, and political structure, Trott stated unequivocally: "Germany must be able to satisfy the desire of the European peoples as a whole that another war amongst them is ruled out as a possibility."

Within such a constructive program an important part was assigned to the United States; not that of a formal mediation or a two-sided guarantee, which was not feasible, as Trott well knew, but that of

"bringing moral weight to bear upon the European situation. . . ."
"If it were felt all over Europe, in the Allied countries as well as in
Germany, that the authority of the United States is backing the effort of devising a fair and durable peace settlement, this would be a
most substantial aid in setting people's minds to work in constructive directions." Trott even envisaged the possibility of the Allied
governments outlining a rational basis for a negotiated peace and
giving a solemn promise to the American people and its government
"that they will fight for and stick by their declared war aims."

There is much in this memorandum which mirrors a situation,
when the war was only two months old and Nazi Germany and Soviet Russia were allies. It was the phase of the "phony war" when
return to sanity still seemed possible. And the desire for a positive
concept of a German and European future was the pivotal point in
Trott's proposals. Such a concept would provide, in his view, decisive support for the German opposition, by giving the lie to Hitler's
propaganda of an anti-German "war of extermination"; and it would
strengthen all rational and sound elements against the nihilistic and
destructive forces in Europe. How far Trott went in personal comments on the changes required in Germany, besides restoration of
the Versailles frontiers, cannot be specified. Nor can the response
which he found be described in more than general terms. It must
suffice to quote Mr. Alexander B. Maley's summary.[19] "Von Trott's
efforts," he says, "were reinforced by other prominent refugees, including Dr. Heinrich Brüning, Catholic pre-Nazi German Chancellor, who visited the White House for this purpose in December 1939.
President Roosevelt at first showed interest in the appeal to support
the German underground but soon, apparently on the advice of men

[19] *Loc. cit.* It may be mentioned that one month later President Roosevelt said
to Sumner Welles "that his obligation to the American people made it imperative for him to leave no stone unturned" (*The Time for Decision*, p. 73). Thus
Trott's attempt was followed by Sumner Welles' mission which kept, of course,
strictly within official channels and set some hope (if any) upon Mussolini. The
discouraging effect which this procedure had upon the German opposition has
been referred to.

138

close to him, discouraged further contacts. Von Trott was even denounced as a Nazi agent, which is bitterly ironical in view of the sequel."

Thus the attempt of this "noble and idealistic young German" (F. Morley) resulted only in providing Washington with a good deal of information. Otherwise it failed completely. Whatever the practical value and the feasibility of the suggestions offered, the refusal to have anything to do with, or to give the mildest sort of sympathy to, a well-credited anti-Nazi was very distinct and set a discouraging precedent. Trott returned via Japan and continued his clandestine work. He was hanged in 1944.

In spite of this failure, the opposition, in November, 1941, made another effort to establish an official contact with the United States while there was still peace, a precarious peace, between the two countries. In this case, the approach was indirect, but aimed at reaching a permanent liaison. Among Americans in Berlin, the one who knew probably more about the true situation than anybody else (certainly more than Mr. William L. Shirer) was Mr. Louis P. Lochner.[20] For many years he had been head of the Berlin office of the Associated Press. Having attended gatherings of resistance elements before, he was taken one night to the meeting of a group of "12–15 idealistic men," as he calls them. The group consisted of representatives of the General Federation of Free Trade Unions and the Christian Trade Unions, of the Confessing Church, of the former Centrist, Democratic, Social-Democratic and German People's political parties, and of one confidant each of Admiral Canaris and of Colonel General Beck. It may be noted that the very composition of this group (probably a sort of "steering committee") is an interesting evidence of the extent as well as the coherence of the opposition, and corroborates what has been derived on that score from other sources of information.

The meeting took place in the home of attorney Joseph Wirmer,

[20] Mr. Lochner has kindly permitted the author to make use of the following facts and has checked upon their authenticity.

a former Centrist deputy, and Jakob Kaiser, the afore-mentioned leader of the Christian Trade Unions, stood out as the most impressive figure. There was among the members of the group a general conviction that America would be in the war before long. As they were discussing the regime to be substituted for Hitler's totalitarianism, and as they all agreed upon the tremendous power and influence of the United States, Mr. Lochner was asked to make every effort, on his return, to see President Roosevelt, to inform him personally of the movement within Germany to unseat the Nazi regime, and to get a reply from him as to what sort of political setup in the Reich would appear acceptable. In fact, Mr. Lochner was presented with a "code" to make direct radio communication possible between the American President and the conspirators.

When, after five months of internment, Mr. Lochner returned to Washington in June, 1942, he tried of course to discharge the mission which had been entrusted to him. After several attempts to see the President had failed, he put his request in writing, stating exactly why he desired a personal interview. The reply which he received was negative, and suggested that he desist because of the "most embarrassing" nature of his request. It took Mr. Lochner some time to realize that this refusal was not accidental, but part of an official policy, of an attitude not only of withholding encouragement or advice requested by the German opposition, not only of rejecting an opportunity which might have led to an important contact, but according to which even a mere recognition of the fact that elements of opposition were in existence in Germany, capable of and prepared for taking over, and the offer of more intimate information about this fact, were obviously felt to be "most embarrassing."

The third attempt to reach an understanding, or at least a basis for a certain co-operation, ended equally in failure. Reference has already been made to a meeting of the Bishop of Chichester with two German pastors in Stockholm in May, 1942. The first to arrive was Dr. Hans Schönfeld, who worked for the World Council of Churches, but also had some official relation with the Nazi Church government.

The Bishop therefore kept on his guard.[21] He felt himself on absolutely sure ground, however, with the second emissary, Pastor Dietrich Bonhoeffer, formerly in charge of the German Church in London. The Bishop knew Bonhoeffer personally and knew that he had all along been working for the Brethren's Council in the Confessing Church. The son of a leading German psychiatrist, Bonhoeffer had been principal of an underground theological seminary, and deeply engaged in political activities. About his uncompromising attitude there was not the slightest doubt. When at an opposition meeting in 1940, of which the Bishop of Chichester had learned, it was proposed to postpone further action in order to avoid giving Hitler the character of a martyr, Bonhoeffer replied, in words which have been partly quoted in another connection: "If we claim to be Christians, there is no room for expediency. Hitler is the Anti-Christ. Therefore we must go on with our work and eliminate him whether he be successful or not."

Bonhoeffer thus stands out as a foremost representative of those who did not hesitate to carry the moral dilemma through to a radical solution—one which was not laid upon the conscience of resisters in any other country. At a secret church meeting at Geneva in 1941 he had said: "I pray for the defeat of my nation. Only in defeat can we atone for the terrible crimes we have committed against Europe and the world."[22] A man with these convictions fitted ideally into the framework of the Intelligence Service (*Abwehr*). Together with his brother Claus, a lawyer, and with his two brothers-in-law, Dr. Ruediger Schleicher and Dr. Hans von Dohnanyi, he worked under General Oster.[23] It was with "papers prepared by the Abwehr" that

[21] About Schönfeld's sympathy with the Confessing Church, however, there was no doubt, and Dulles (*op. cit.*, p. 117), who later co-operated with him in Switzerland, gives him a very clean bill of health. The main source for the following is the report of the Bishop of Chichester, "The Background of the Hitler Plot," *The Contemporary Review*, September, 1945, pp. 203–8.

[22] Dulles, *op. cit.*, p. 116.

[23] All four members of the Bonhoeffer family were executed or murdered. Dohnanyi was the first to be trapped when, in late 1943, the Gestapo discovered his involvement in foreign currency transactions ("the purpose of which was to

he came to Stockholm.[24] He had a spiritual as well as an official authority for his message.

What impressed the Bishop all the more was the fact that both pastors said materially the same thing, though neither knew of the other's coming. Schönfeld first informed him of the strength and composition of the oppositional groups, of their progress in organization and preparation during the last six months. The purpose, he said, was the destruction of the whole Nazi regime, including Hitler, Himmler, Göring, and Goebbels, as well as the leaders of Gestapo, SS and SA. A new government was to be established, with all oppositional groups represented, and with a program which he outlined in a written memorandum. It envisaged: 1. a largely decentralized Germany, "governed by law and social justice"; 2. an economic reconstruction along "truly socialist lines, instead of self-sufficient autarchy"; and close co-operation between free nations, their interdependence becoming "the strongest possible guarantee against self-reactionary European militarism"; 3. a European federation of free states, including a free Polish and a free Czech nation. The federation should have "a common executive, under the authority of which a European army would be created for the permanent ordering of European security."

Whether this can be regarded as an "official" offer of the German opposition may be questioned, though definite similarities exist with the Kreisau ideas, as well as, to some extent, with those of Goerdeler. Common to most of the German oppositional groups was certainly the conclusion to which Schönfeld came: "The foundation principles of national and social life within this federation of free European

provide for people who had to take refuge abroad," as Mr. Dulles states, *op. cit.*, p. 79). This gave Himmler the opportunity for a decisive blow against the Intelligence Service.

[24] *Ibid.*, p. 78. The only comment which Gisevius (*op. cit.*, p. 449) has on the mission of Bonhoeffer is that it was "intended to offset any false impression produced by the negotiations in the Vatican." Again it is obvious that while having no authentic knowledge, he tries to find an "interesting" angle.

nations should be orientated or re-orientated towards the fundamental principles of Christian Faith and Life."

With Bonhoeffer, the Bishop had a more intimate conversation, in which he received reassuring, and one may add, absolutely correct information about the chief conspirators, their character, and their political leanings. When Schönfeld joined them, it was obvious that Bonhoeffer took the more vigorous view. He did not enter upon concrete stipulations. "We do not want to escape repentance," he said. "Our action must be understood as an act of repentance." The Bishop of Chichester emphasized the necessity of such a declaration of repentance, "and this was accepted." It was also understood that "the Americans and the Russians would both have to be brought in and that Allied armies would have to occupy Berlin." While the Bishop warned against being very hopeful he declared himself willing to transmit the message.

This leads to the practical point. Schönfeld had stated that in view of the immense danger to be incurred by the conspirators it was extremely important to know "whether the Allies' attitude to a Germany purged of Hitler would be different from their attitude to a Germany under Hitler. The alternative seemed further destruction and chaos and increasing nihilism as the war went on." The Bishop himself summed the message up in 2 questions:

"1. Would the Allied Governments, once the whole Hitler regime was overthrown, be willing to treat with a bona fide German Government for such a peace settlement as that described . . . including the withdrawal of all German forces from occupied countries, and reparation for damage, and to say so privately to an authorized representative of the German opposition?[25]—Or

"2. Could the Allies make a public announcement in the clearest terms to a similar effect?"

On his return to London the Bishop placed a detailed account and a written memorandum before Mr. Anthony Eden. He was told that

[25] As a possible intermediary Adam v. Trott was mentioned, *op. cit.*, p. 207.

some of the names which Bonhoeffer had mentioned were known at the Foreign Office and that other peace feelers had reached him via neutral countries. Of course, no negotiations were possible apart from the Americans and the Russians, but Mr. Eden declared that he would consider the matter. On July 17, the Bishop was informed that "no action could be taken."

It is not the purpose of this study to enter into a full discussion of the negative attitude which the Western Allies maintained through the years. One can think of a number of motives. The diplomatic angle, the fear of compromising the grand alliance, is obvious, though it would not necessarily have demanded a policy of "no action." Moreover, such a viewpoint cannot possibly apply to Trott's sounding which was undertaken during the phase of Nazi-Soviet liaison. Nor do the overtures made through Mr. Lochner, which simply asked for advice, or those of the two pastors who understood that both the Americans and the Russians would have to be brought in and Berlin be jointly occupied, bear out a German intention of splitting the Allied front. They rather bear out, as did Trott's proposal, a fear of chaos and nihilism. Perhaps this can be better appreciated today than it was in 1940 and 1942.

Another possible motive suggests itself. Was not the somewhat surprising concern of Germans about the reconstruction and regeneration of Europe and about a durable international order to be suspected as a peace offensive of militarists and nationalists who wanted to save some of the Hitlerian gains, before it was too late? There is no doubt that Von Hassell and Goerdeler (though not the cool-headed Colonel General Beck) were under illusions regarding "national" aims which might be acceptable in the early years. In February, 1940,[26] Hassell transmitted to an English emissary a draft which stressed a "permanent pacification of Europe" and certain principles to be recognized by all European states. He enumerated the re-establishment of an independent Poland, of a Czech republic, general reduction of armament, and the application of Christian ethics, of jus-

[26] *Diaries*, pp. 117–18.

tice, of social welfare, of effective popular control as "fundamental elements of public life." But he also demanded that the union of Austria and the Sudeten with the Reich be left "out of any discussion" and that the German-Polish frontiers be "more or less identical" with the frontier of 1914. In a proposal which he is said to have conveyed to Washington in autumn, 1941,[27] he obviously had given up the idea of claiming the Sudeten area, and as to the settlement of the Polish corridor issue, he suggested an exchange which would give to Poland an outlet to the sea through incorporation of four eastern districts of East Prussia. Of Goerdeler it is known that he thought at times even of regaining some colonies and adding to the Reich the German part of South Tirol.[28]

But on the other hand, it has been shown that Von Trott, as early as October, 1939, suggested a guarantee of the Versailles frontiers. It may have been surprising when he added in his memorandum that "nationalism of the kind which finds its most extreme expression in Nazidom has been distinctly on the downgrade in Europe for some time." This seems to be a paradox, but makes sense in view of the fact that the Hitler movement, in spite of its criticism of nineteenth-century politics, was in many ways only the belated climax of that period of secularism as well as of nationalism. The truth of the contention that some of these nineteenth-century tendencies were actually on the "downgrade" could be experienced by anyone who, before 1933, was in contact with the truly progressive forces, neoconservative and socialist, which struggled for new forms of international co-operation in Central Europe—with those forces, for example,

[27] This information is contained in Mr. Alexander B. Maley's article, *op. cit.*, p. 7. Hassell's diaries only indicate (p. 217, October 4, 1941) that according to "Stallforth" the "proposition" had been well received in America and that a meeting was suggested with "an authorized person" in Lisbon. Hassell himself was skeptical about this information. What the content of the proposal was, cannot be ascertained; it can hardly be identical with the one which, according to Mr. Maley, reached Washington only shortly before Pearl Harbor.

[28] Pechel, *op. cit.*, p. 215. Evidences of a retrospective character are also contained in Goerdeler's letter of March 26, 1943, to the generals (Kaiser diary, App.).

which were active in the "International Congress of European Nationalities."[29] Trott himself referred to the fact that Hitler had to let the war "slide in by the back door," and that the German people in 1938–39, were certainly as little enthusiastic about war as any other nation. In addition, there was nothing "nationalistic" or "militaristic" in the plans of the Kreisau circle, for which Trott was the spokesman in matters of foreign policy.[30] Nor could Bonhoeffer, the agent of the Abwehr, with his insistence upon a "declaration of repentance," be suspected on that score. Moreover, the British Foreign Office certainly knew what the Abwehr was doing for the common cause of humanity. And it was also known in London and probably in Washington as well, what the attitude of military men such as Beck and Witzleben or of diplomats such as Weizsäcker had been in 1938, and how little they conformed to a conventional pattern of militarism and nationalism.

Another fact that could not be known, but must in fairness be added, is that Goerdeler, the presumptive political leader of a new government, was also engaged in plans, which went far beyond national interests. His "World Peace Program" of 1939[31] was only a first instance. The whole concept of a decentralized and federalized Germany and of a state with a corporative structure meant a breaking away from nineteenth-century tenets and an abandonment of old ideas of political sovereignty. This was a trend of thought common to almost all groups of the German opposition. Along this line, Goerdeler set up a draft[32] which envisaged, side by side with a federalized Germany, several other unions or federations in Europe: an Eastern European (Poland, Lithuania, Latvia, Estonia), a Southern

[29] Cf. C. A. Macartney, *National State and National Minorities*, p. 394; also the author's articles on "The Baltic Provinces," *Journal of Central European Affairs*, July, 1944, pp. 138–40, and on "Frontiers and Mass Migrations in Eastern Central Europe," *Review of Politics*, January, 1946, pp. 65–66.

[30] Gerstenmaier in his letter about the Conference of January, 1943, (*op. cit.*) mentions this fact.

[31] See p. 131, n. 3.

[32] See abstracts in Pechel, *op. cit.*, pp. 213–20.

146

European, a Balkan, a Scandinavian union, and so forth. He likewise thought in terms of a European union as being a member of a world union, of Europe approaching economic unification and being provided with an interunion police force; with a president to be elected for four years by the council, with a council composed of two representatives of each of the several unions, and with a union parliament, to which each of the federative parliaments should delegate five or ten deputies.

It is not, however, the detail of such proposals but their general character that interests us here. Nobody can deny that within the German opposition a body of inter-European and international thought was alive which commands respect, whatever its practicality. There were men willing to contribute to the security of Europe and the world by fundamentally reducing the danger of a centralized power in the midst of the continent. They probably felt that this was as much a positive effort on their part as would be required: a positive way of atonement; and there were among them ideas under discussion which can hardly be characterized as a mere cloak for national or social interests. Nor were they merely conjured up under the pressure of an extreme emergency; they had grown out of genuine German traditions of pre-Hitlerian times.

Whether or not, or to what extent, this could be realized in London or Washington, may be considered as an open question. Certain it is that to acknowledge any possible and genuine contribution of Germans toward a lasting peace, or to face any kind of negotiation with a bona-fide German partner was felt to be "most embarrassing." This would have meant the reversal of a line of propaganda which insisted upon the identification of Nazis with Germans and upon the thesis that, in particular, German military leaders (militarists), who undoubtedly formed a sector of the opposition, were "just as bad as Hitler's outfit." Such recognition of partnership, moreover, even if it were to be only theoretical for the time being, might have led to a commitment recalling the "Pre-Armistice Agreement" of 1918.

And here another motive appears which has greatly influenced the negative attitude of the Western powers. Not only should defeat be brought home and the military be forced to sign the capitulation themselves. There would have been no serious difficulty in putting that through, as the attitude of Beck or Witzleben clearly indicates. But in addition, any commitment was to be avoided that could justify a later revisionist claim on the German part, or give to a later demagogue and "rabble-rouser" the opportunity to charge the Allies with cheating. Much better not to enter into any agreements at all. In view of one of the historic lessons which the failure of Versailles seemed to convey, and the oblivion into which many other "lessons" had fallen, this was, perhaps, an understandable trend of thought, but one bound to result in a self-defeating policy.

A prelude to such an effect can already be seen in the sad story of the Atlantic Charter. It was proclaimed in August, 1941, and promised in its first three clauses a policy of "no aggrandizement, territorial or other," a policy of abstaining from "territorial changes that do not accord with the freely expressed wishes of the peoples concerned," and a policy of respecting "the right of all peoples to choose" their own form of government. On this basis the United Nations convened in January, 1942. But by no means was the proclamation to imply, as Mr. Churchill announced, a commitment towards the enemy countries. As at that time hardly anybody would have admitted that occupied countries (like the Baltic states) or parts of Allied countries (like Poland) might be in danger of annexation, it is very difficult to imagine to what other but the enemy countries the three pledges were actually meant to apply. Thus the Atlantic Charter was emptied of its main content long before its ideals became a matter of melancholic reminiscence.

Whatever the respective weight of the various motives in determining the Allied policy toward the German opposition, all approaches and peace moves were doomed to end in failure. This situation received the official seal when in January, 1943, at Casablanca, the formula of "unconditional surrender" was agreed upon.

Its bearing upon our subject is the last point which this discussion has to consider.

2

"*Unconditional Surrender*"

If one man can be singled out who had specific reason to complain of the Casablanca formula, it was, paradoxically enough, the chief agent of American Intelligence on the European continent, Mr. Allen Welsh Dulles. As was mentioned before, he came to Switzerland in November, 1942. One of his main objectives was to gauge the situation in Germany and to furnish all possible information about anti-Nazi movements and underground activities in that country. He certainly did a brilliant job. He established relations not only with well-informed political exiles, with members of international church organizations and occasional travelers from Germany, but he also came into close contact with active members of the conspiracy itself—with Gisevius in the first place, with Waetjen, Struenk, and through an intermediary, with Von Trott. In secret codes he sent most valuable reports about the "Breakers," as the conspirators were called in his messages. Aided by Von Gaevernitz, he gave a rather comprehensive analysis of the situation; in fact, eight days before July 20, he was able to predict "dramatic developments."[33]

It is of interest to ask what the reaction was of those men to whom this information was passed on? Or as Mr. Harold C. Deutsch puts it, more drastically:[34] "In which Washington wastebasket did it land?" Mr. Dulles, naturally, treats the lack of official response, disappointing though it must have been to him, with great restraint. But he speaks in no uncertain terms of the fact that at Casablanca, Allied policy toward Germany was "frozen" into the formula of unconditional surrender.[35] In fact, the proclamation of January, 1943, not only

[33] Dulles, *op. cit.*, p. 140.
[34] *American Historical Review*, January, 1948, p. 338.
[35] Dulles, *op. cit.*, p. 132.

149

furnished Dr. Goebbels with considerable ammunition, but by the same token, deprived Mr. Dulles of effective means of psychological warfare—of those means which the Soviets, for example, handled cleverly through Stalin's speeches and the so-called "Free Germany Committee." Mr. Dulles states with regret that, while even London eventually made some innocuous appeals to the German opposition, nothing of this nature was done in Washington.[36]

Such a complaint, however, moves entirely within the limits of tactical considerations; it criticizes the negative propaganda value of the formula. Of a similar technical character was the military criticism voiced in General Eisenhower's entourage.[37] After all, "no surrender was ever made without some conditions," as Captain Harry C. Butcher noted in his *Diary*. Or, as a later entry reads: "There is a feeling that at Casablanca the President and the Prime Minister, more likely the former, seized on Grant's famous terms without realizing the full implications to the enemy. . . . Our psychological experts believe we would be wiser if we created a mood of acceptance of surrender in the German army. . . ." It is quite possible that this technical mistake and the lack of flexibility deriving therefrom have considerably delayed total victory and the end of the war. Looked at from the same tactical angle, the policy of unconditional surrender certainly made it harder for the German opposition to win over reluctant generals.

But the problem has a broader aspect—one involving the matter of principles as well as that of tactics. And it is only against this background that one can fully understand what the "freezing" of Allied policies meant for the German opposition to Hitler. It may very well be that the Casablanca formula was more or less an improvisation, primarily meant to be, as Mr. R. G. Swing indicates, a "morale

[36] *Ibid.*, p. 141.
[37] The following quotations and evaluations are taken from an article by Raymond G. Swing, "Unconditional Surrender," *Atlantic Monthly*, September, 1947, pp. 38–40. Entries of Capt. Harry C. Butcher in his diary of August 12, 1943, and of April 14, 1944, respectively. Cf. Butcher, *My Three Years with Eisenhower* (New York, 1947), pp. 386, 518.

builder," and adopted in 1943 for the purpose of giving the Allies a "shot in the arm." It may also very well be that the policy of unconditional surrender did not yet imply the idea of a Carthaginian peace in the literal sense of the word. The Conference of Teheran, which envisaged the cutting-off of Germany's "bread basket" and the dumping of millions of expellees into a country reduced by 25 per cent, was still ten months ahead. And the Morgenthau plan, which on top of that looked "forward to converting Germany into a country primarily agricultural and pastoral in character," was not endorsed before Quebec, in September, 1944. Even then, as we know, Winston Churchill was reluctant to subscribe to this insanity, and President Roosevelt confessed soon afterward, in a conversation with the Secretary of War, that "he did not know how he had initialed that particular language in the Quebec agreement." It must have been done, he said, "without much thought."[38] It is admittedly difficult to imagine, that forces which worked towards such a destructive and self-defeating policy, that fears of a "soft peace," that blind hatred and the wish to dispose once and for all of Germany as a political and economic power, were not already active in earlier years; but there is no reason to assume their direct influence upon the Casablanca formula.

Certain it is, however, that "unconditional surrender" epitomized a negative attitude which had been on record before and which, as far as principles go, was meant to keep the dictatorial authority of the victors free of obligations. By refusing to acknowledge any German partner, it pointed logically toward a vacuum. In fact, this consequence has only been avoided in the case of Japan when the formula was eventually discarded. In the case of Germany, the policy of "no advance commitment" prevailed; it ended, indeed, in the most complete military victory. But just as this policy had defeated the idealism of the Atlantic Charter, it defeated itself by resulting in the heaviest possible commitment. As there was to be no function of a German government, except that of surrendering unconditionally, all

[38] James F. Byrnes, *Speaking Frankly* (New York, 1947), p. 186.

responsibility, in fact, an "unconditional responsibility," fell upon the Allied governments. As Mr. Victor Gollancz puts it: "The Germans were required to place themselves entirely in our hands. . . . If that does not impose a special obligation on a nation that calls itself civilized, what does?"[39] Thus by trying to avoid any obligation, actually an obligation of the most categorical character was incurred.

It is obvious, of course, that no dealings whatsoever were possible with a Nazi or Nazi-appointed government. But while this very fact might have made the German opposition an asset, not only for the purposes of propaganda and psychological warfare but in terms of constructive policy, it happened, as has been aptly pointed out,[40] that "the Allied leaders, like their Nazi opponents, [became] victims of their own war propaganda, which insisted that all Germans were in the same boat." In consequence it also happened—or one may say—a bitter irony of history willed, that the Western powers practically co-operated with Hitler's policy, not only with his heaping of abuse upon the conspirators, but also with his deliberate nihilism, with his policy of producing a maximum of destruction and leaving chaos behind. Desiring sincerely to implant democracy they found themselves inheriting a dictatorial rule and many of its arbitrary methods.

The attitude of the Western Allies towards the German opposition is one part only of this large complex of problems, but a highly symptomatic one. When Mr. Churchill, on August 2, 1944, ten days after the Twentieth of July, declared in the House of Commons,[41] that this was simply a case of the highest personalities in the German Reich "murdering each other," he acted as much against better knowledge and fell in as much with Goebbels and Hitler as did the American Office of War Information. Such propaganda was bound to backfire. As a matter of fact, it was not the existence, but rather the absence, of an anti-Nazi shadow government which eventually

[39] *Our Threatened Values*, p. 193.
[40] By Mr. Harold C. Deutsch, *op. cit.*, p. 338.
[41] Hansard, *Parliamentary Debates*, Vol. 402, p. 1487.

would prove to be "most embarrassing." Its original members, of course, had meanwhile been killed off. But with an official thesis and a policy of indoctrination which still, for many months to come, maintained that all Germans were basically untrustworthy, it was very difficult to activate the forces which had gathered in the German opposition. Thus it seems safe to say that a good deal of self-created perplexities followed from the negative attitude embedded in the formula of unconditional surrender.

On the other hand, of course, Casablanca cut off any hope for a bearable peace which the German Resistance might still have had and made the usefulness of further contacts with the West highly questionable. While up to this time there is simply no evidence which bears out the reproach that the conspirators tried to split up the Allied front, it seems as if now their own front was splitting up into a Western and an Eastern faction. As Von Gaevernitz stated after a secret meeting with Von Trott:[42] "Constructive ideas and plans for the re-building of postwar Germany constantly come from Russia" whereas "the democratic countries offer nothing concerning the future of Central Europe.... Socialist leaders in Germany emphasize the importance of filling this vacuum.... If it is permitted to continue, German labor leaders fear that in spite of military victory the democracies may lose the peace and the present dictatorship in Central Europe be exchanged for a new one."

This analysis has all the ring of verity and prophecy, but it certainly does not bear out an unqualified turn to the East. On the whole, the conspiracy, including its trade unionists and even the radicals, was in the political sense of the word decidedly Western, as has previously been pointed out. It has also been mentioned that at the end of 1942 some socialist members vetoed action or advocated its postponement, until the Western Allies had landed on the Continent. No doubt, the German anti-Nazis would have generally preferred to see enemy victory and German capitulation come about in the West first. To assume, however, that after that had happened, Beck or Goerdeler

[42] Dulles, *op. cit.*, p. 137–38.

would have thought of being able to continue the war in the East or even to find Western support for such action, is to underestimate their intellectual as well as their moral caliber. The Western orientation in the military sense was a matter, not of playing off one side against the other, but one of preference, based on the expectation of some more "civilized" treatment of women, for example, or a greater respect for basic human rights on the part of Western soldiers; it was one may say, a matter of preference for Europe as against Asia. In May, 1944, proposals were made through Gisevius for opening the way to Allied landings in France and northern Germany and for the descent of three airborne Allied divisions upon Berlin.[43]

But the silence of the Western statesmen combined with aerial terror from the West and, in addition, the absolute necessity to end the war, encouraged approaches to the Soviets. Stalin, after all, had expressed the strongest possible distinction between Nazis and Germans. Von Trott seems to have been engaged in negotiations with Madame Kollontay, the Russian envoy at Stockholm, in the summer of 1944. And the former Ambassador in Moscow, Count Werner von der Schulenburg advocated coming to terms with Stalin first, in order to reach "general peace" (Dulles). That is why he was kept as an alternate to Hassell as presumptive Foreign Minister.

But these counsels of despair should not be mistaken for an Eastern orientation in a pro-Soviet sense. Mr. Dulles, on the basis of Gisevius' misleading information, unfortunately has obscured this issue to a considerable extent. While he states repeatedly that there was eventually no dissent regarding Eastern or Western orientation within the conspiracy and that all began to realize it would have to be "unconditional and simultaneous surrender," he still maintains that they disagreed, "whether to look eastward toward Communism or westward towards democracy," and that this threat to their unity continued to "the very last minute."[44] Moreover, he blurs the pic-

[43] *Ibid.*, p. 139.
[44] *Ibid.*, pp. 139, 140, 165, 173–74. Particularly contradictory are the statements on pages 140 and 173.

ture by calling the Westerners "military" and "revolutionary" and the Easterners "evolutionary," because they were allegedly against the plot and believed "Hitler and his gang should, before history and the German people, drink the dregs of defeat."[45] In truth, the Kreisau circle, while by no means advocating inactivity, was certainly more "revolutionary," at least in economic and social matters, than the other non-Communist elements of the opposition. They were prepared to take the Soviet experiment very seriously in many respects. What they really stood for, however, and what their anti-Western tendency really implied, was unmistakably expressed by Trott zu Solz at the time of Casablanca, and it is hard to see how his words could be misunderstood as pro-Soviet. In fact, they give so important a clue to the position which Trott and his group occupied between West and East, that it seems desirable to quote them at some length.[46]

Von Trott started from the disappointing experiences made in all conversation with the West and from the "failure of the Western powers to understand that the Germans are themselves an oppressed people who live in an occupied country and that tremendous risks are taken by the opposition in continuing its activity." "As a result," he said, "the opposition believes the Anglo-Saxon countries are filled with bourgeois prejudice and pharisaic theorizing. There is a strong temptation to turn east. The reason for the eastward orientation is the belief in the possibility of fraternization between the Russian and German peoples, although not between the present governments. Both have broken with bourgeois ideology, both have suffered deeply, both desire a radical solution of social problems which transcends national limits, both are in the process of returning to the spiritual (but not the ecclesiastical) traditions of Christianity. The German soldier has respect, not hatred, for the Russian. The opposition believes that the decisive development in Europe will take place in the social, not in the military, realm. When the cam-

[45] *Ibid.*, pp. 134–35.
[46] *Ibid.*, p. 132.

paign in Russia stalls, after the German army has been thrown back, a revolutionary situation may arise on both sides. Fraternization between Germans and imported foreign workers is also an important element. Hitler has been forced to play up to the laboring classes and has given them an increasingly strong position; the bourgeoisie and intellectuals and generals are of less and less importance. Hitler will fall, and the brotherhood of the oppressed is the basis upon which a completely new Europe will be built."

It was this visionary idea of "a brotherhood of the oppressed" to which Stauffenberg likewise adhered, however slim its basis may appear. And his attempt to save the Russian volunteers, who served on the German side, from being used as cannon fodder and as tools of German or Russian nationalism, brings this underlying concept to full evidence.[47] It also brings out the innermost impulse which gives to the German opposition an exceptional rank; its principled stand against totalitarianism of any kind, its insistence upon the leading ideas of European civilization, upon human dignity, upon the spiritual traditions of Christianity and the basic values of man's existence, as against the forces of dehumanized social and political systems. To stress this, however, is also to state that the German opposition found little support in so-called realities. It was a vanguard fighting against hope and with no national or social rewards within its reach.

In fact, such was the situation after January, 1943, whatever outlets were tried or whatever desperate efforts were made. Basically there was no chance and nothing left but to do what was necessary. Mr. Dulles sums that up quite correctly when he states[48] that the

[47] This is the leading and undoubtedly genuine theme of the romanticized story which Karl Michel has built around Stauffenberg. See p. 72, n. 49; p. 129, n. 170. It seems also incontestable that there had been a large amount of fraternization between German soldiers and the Russian people in the interval between the departure of the Communist commissars and the arrival of the Gestapo or the SS troops. Interesting material on that aspect can be found in a manuscript, "Impressions and Thoughts of an Average Russian Woman," which has reached this country.

[48] Op. cit., p. 146.

conspirators "would have to go ahead, if they chose, not in the hope of securing better peace terms, but solely because the duty to cleanse their own house was an absolute one. It was not conditional upon the help and promises of others." Whereas all Undergrounds throughout Europe had received vast material and psychological support and had very concrete rewards within their reach, the German alone was entirely left to its own resources. These were military only at the surface; fundamentally they were spiritual. It is on this ground that murder could be conceived as religious duty, as a duty of clearing the German name and freeing the world from the evil, a liberation to be effected by Germans themselves. The words of Von Tresckow have been quoted which pointed that out. In the same vein it was that the former Secretary of State Erwin Planck said: "The attempt has to be tried solely because of the moral rehabilitation of Germany, no matter whether an improvement of Germany's prospects can be reached thereby."[49] This had not been the stand in 1938 or at the beginning of the war, when it still seemed possible to save parts of the political and social structure of prewar Europe. But eventually Casablanca was answered with another "unconditional" attitude, that of attack upon a regime, whether or not its overthrow promised a bearable rather than an unbearable peace. It actually promised nothing, except a shortening of the war which might save innumerable lives and spare the whole of Europe and of Western culture the deepest downfall into chaos and nihilism which was still to come.

[49] Franz Reuter, *Der 20. Juli* (Berlin, 1946), p. 31.

SUMMARY

In trying to establish a certain balance sheet, many questions have to be left open. Not only factual questions, which may never be fully cleared up, but also questions of judgment which transcend the historian's competence and probably that of mortal man altogether. After the events of a decade, certainly after those of the last three or four years, it requires, to say the least, a certain robustness of conscience to place oneself in the judge's seat, and it requires a good deal of complacency to single out one nation for guilt, or to give a verdict on its "moral rehabilitation." If for no other reason, it is out of respect for the gravity and the comprehensive character of the problems involved that this study was not and is not meant to be a plea for the defense. No competence is arrogated here which would enable us to decide whether or not the existence, the range, and the character of the German opposition to Hitler justifies extenuation or can be accepted as indemnity. It may suffice to note, and this is perhaps more important than any statement one might make today from behind a writing desk, that the leading men of the conspiracy itself, churchmen and laymen alike, in the midst of turbulent events and emotional stress, lived and died for the idea of atonement. In a farewell letter, which Goerdeler wrote in prison, he gave expression to the same line of thought to be found in many other documents of the German resistance. He concluded the letter with the words:[1] "May the world accept our martyrdom as penance in behalf of the German people."

It is not to consider how this plea may be answered in the realm of metaphysics or politics; it is rather for the sake of historical justice that this study was begun. One of its concerns, therefore, was to bring out facts which are either unknown to the public or have not been presented so far in their entirety, in their relation to, and integration with, each other—facts which need to be placed in their proper setting and to be examined critically as far as the underlying

[1] The quotation is taken from the memorandum of Frau Goerdeler.

158

sources of information are concerned. All this is a legitimate province of the historian. And the hope may be expressed, that within the confines of fact-finding, a broad area may now be regarded as secure and above the distorting influence of party strife, passion, resentment, and political propaganda of whatever sort. While the intention of this study was not to replace one legend by another, historical judgment nonetheless is bound to move far away from a previously accepted picture, which hitherto has been only incompletely and inadequately revised.

A few results of this "revisionist" character may be briefly summarized. The German opposition to Hitler was not only much broader than has been conceded so far, but also more extensive than could have been expected under conditions of terror. Not only did it move through various stages of nonconformity: from antagonism muted by prison walls and the silence of a potential opposition, from humanitarian protest and clandestine aid to victims of persecution, to sabotage by the illegals and their subversive activities, to spiritual attack upon the very essence of totalitarianism, to active planning and political resistance. In addition, it can be stated that the German opposition reached definite form long before the war, and that it reached its first climax in an attempt to prevent war. It was not the threat of defeat which made the opposition articulate; on the contrary, some of its leading elements were convinced that Hitler's victory would be the greatest of all possible catastrophes—a victory of "the archenemy of the whole world", of the Antichrist; they worked against this danger at a time when a German military victory still seemed probable. While the spearhead of the opposition was military, as it is bound to be under a totalitarian system, its "body and soul" were civilian. While the conspiracy was directed by top men, it comprised among them all elements of society: labor and church, business and intellectual, as well as aristocratic and military elements. It furnished from its ranks a roster of personalities who were able and prepared to take over the government of Germany in the center of the state as well as on the provincial and municipal level; it was even in a position to send "authorized representatives" abroad. While the opposition, for obvious reasons, could not be a mass movement, it was equipped with a network of cells and reached far down into the small communities. Moreover, it had a concrete program, not binding for all component elements, but one to which a broad coalition of oppositional forces adhered, and one far exceeding merely negative ends.

It is with the analysis of this positive program, of the motives, the concrete purposes, and the leading ideas of the German opposition that the historian's task turns from mere fact-finding to interpretation—a more important and, of course, a more delicate task. Again, it is to be hoped that some of the gravest distortions can be regarded as definitely disposed of, and some of the major biases at least opened up for frank and honest debate.

By contrast, we might remember to what lengths these distortions and biases have actually gone. It can hardly be denied that official pronouncements, once they were forced to admit the existence of a German opposition, gave out a caricature and insisted on the militaristic bogey in a way which suggests the strangest sort of alliance, that between Hitlerian and democratic propaganda. Thus the ground was prepared for fantastic repercussions.

It may suffice to quote two press comments[2] by which the meaning of the Twentieth of July was explained to the American public. On August 9, the *New York Times* stated that the details of the plot were reminiscent of "the atmosphere of a gangster's lurid underworld," rather than of that atmosphere which one would normally expect "within an officer's corps and a civilized government." For a year, some of the highest officers of the German army, the *Times* remarked almost reproachfully, had been planning "to kidnap or kill the head of the German state and Commander in Chief

[2] The following quotations are taken from an article by Robert Ingrim, "Diplomacy in Ideological Fetters" (*Thought*, March, 1947, pp. 44–45). The article has meanwhile been published in Zürich as a pamphlet under the title: *Aussenpolitik mit falschen Begriffen*. It contains also some very pertinent remarks on European conservatism as a barrier against totalitarianism.

of the Army." Eventually they carried out their plan "by means of a bomb, the typical weapon of the underworld. . . ." A few days earlier (August 2), the *Herald Tribune* had written: "If Hitlerism has begun its last stand by destroying the militarist tradition, then it has been doing a large part of the Allies' work for them." And on August 9, the *Herald Tribune* added the following appraisal: "American people as a whole will not feel sorry that the bomb spared Hitler for the liquidation of his generals. They hold no brief for aristocrats as such, especially those given to the goosestep, and when it connives with their plans, to collaboration with low-born, mob-rousing corporals. Let the generals kill the corporal, or vice-versa, preferably both."

There is a considerable distance between the ethics of these editorials and the ethics of those men, many among them officers and aristocrats, who felt it their duty to break through bonds of conventional loyalty and to "kidnap or kill" the head of the state, the supreme commander. While the problem of militarism is not one to be slighted, the bogus theory which has been built around this historical phenomenon carries insupportable generalizations. In view of the evidence available, it would be more appropriate to state that those traditions of a genuine "Prussian militarism" which still existed in Nazi Germany, formed a barrier against nationalist and demagogic excesses, and that it was unfortunate so few of them had survived the "Age of Materialism." However this may be, the leading military and aristocratic members of the conspiracy certainly thought little in terms of a profession or a caste, and very much in terms of restoring human and supranational values. They were fundamentally driven by moral and religious impulses. It does not seem necessary to recapitulate the ideas and actions which bear out this interpretation.

A related interpretative aspect, however, must be briefly touched upon in this summary. It concerns the aristocratic and conservative elements, or the restorative tendencies within the German opposition. The usual sociological approach does not help much in trying to cover these problems, while on the other hand the historical approach is impeded by democratic and egalitarian traditions of two hundred years' standing, and by certain semantic difficulties as well. It is an obvious fact that the terms "liberal" and "conservative" do not have exactly the same meaning in the United States as they do in Europe. This very interesting phenomenon can receive no general treatment here, but is mentioned only with reference to an appraisal of the German opposition. American authors who have written on the subject tend to describe the most energetic anti-Nazis as "liberals"; in European terms, however, they may have been either radical socialists or radical conservatives—that is, opposed in either case, to state tyranny as well as to rugged individualism. There is also a natural inclination to suspect not only "Junkers" but aristocrats and traditionalists in general of reactionary tendencies; whereas, to the Kreisau aristocrats and other conservatives, as well as to their socialist associates, Goerdeler was a reactionary because of his "liberal" leanings toward the nineteenth-century ideal of a competitive society.

This is an unusual terminology, but it can help us to avoid hasty conclusions. Liberals, socialists, and conservatives all contributed to the German opposition. Nor can the resistance be classified as a reactionary movement simply because conservative and aristocratic elements participated in it so extensively. As far as a restorative tendency existed, it pointed rather to a renewal of liberal and middle-class institutions, the social basis of which had largely vanished. On the other hand, the desire to restore the cultural values of Western Europe, to re-establish the dignity of man, or the "proper relationship of responsibility and rights"—all this was eminently conservative. Just as in the religious sphere, genuine conservatism of a political nature regained its traditional stand against the glorification of state or nation, of technology or Mammon, indeed of everything that made man a means to an end.

Thus, everywhere in Europe, among Catholics and Protestants alike, the forces of religious, cultural, and political conservatism revived, once a secularized society was threatened by, or fell victim to, nihilism or fascism. In Germany this became apparent in parts of the youth movement and other neoconservative groups of the twenties. Under the pressure of the Hitler regime these joined with socialist elements in a progressive front directed against the centralistic nation-state, its underlying social and economic system, and other tenets of the preceding century.

In political terms, this meant that the German opposition had no intention of taking up where the Weimar Republic had left off. Their plans pointed, in various shades and degrees, towards a conservative and decentralized democracy with a more or less strong admixture of socialism. They were certainly set against mass democracy. While this may appear "romantic," it is worth while to recall that the founders of the American Republic also believed unqualified majority rule was certain to lead to tyranny. Their system of checks and balances was different from that which the German opposition outlined, but it likewise had aspects of a conservative democracy; and the insistence upon local self-government and decentralization was principally the same. In Germany, this meant going back to soundest traditions. And the opinion may be ventured that there were elements in this body of thought which appear highly preferable to the political setup of democracy which has been reinstituted meanwhile, to the revival of a party bureaucracy which has fewer roots in the country than ever before, and to a large-scale democratic machinery which is bound to operate in an atmosphere of complete unreality.

Likewise, the international ideas of the German opposition are not inconsistent with our direst needs today. It may be noted that their plans for the dissolution of Prussia and the federalization of Germany were not of a negative character, they were not dictated by resentment, they did not merely want to prevent the revival of a great power in the center of Europe, though they acknowledged this as a necessary measure and offered it as a sacrifice to be made by Germany. In addition, they thought in terms of an economically viable, but culturally and politically diversified, Central Europe, of a union of federations as a member of a European and a world federation.

163

But they also knew, as Moltke pointed out, that all this was "less a problem of frontiers and soldiers, of top-heavy organizations or grand plans, than a question of how the picture of man can be restored in the breasts of our fellow citizens." In other words, they knew that all reconstruction, nationally and internationally, was dependent on the rehabilitation of the dignity of man. These were no empty sentences which had been placed before the Bishop of Chichester: "The foundation principles . . . within this federation of free European nations should be orientated or re-orientated towards the fundamental principles of Christian Faith and Life."

It may be that this idealism does not appeal to the neorealists of our days. In truth, though, it may be more realistic than reliance on "soldiers and top-heavy organizations." But whatever the final appraisal, nobody can doubt that under the extraordinary circumstances which prevailed in Germany, an extraordinary group of men emerged who were part of a broader uprising of the human against the subhuman, who represented what may be called a moral elite.

All the more, then, the tragedy of the Twentieth of July stands out in its full perspective. And it may be safe to assume that the *Herald Tribune* was wrong in predicting: "Americans as a whole will not feel sorry that the bomb saved Hitler." A successful attempt, it is true, would have prevented a series of American victories. But it would have spared the lives of millions of soldiers on all fronts, who died during the months from July, 1944, to May, 1945, and those of the masses of civilians who died in extermination camps in Poland or in bombed German cities. In addition, the failure led to the wholesale elimination of German men and women who, like innumerable others, are now sorely missed in the task of reconstruction.

It is impossible to say today, whether the seed which they planted, or out of which they grew themselves, has survived or can be revived in spite of the physical and moral debris which has since been piled up. The Nazi intention certainly was to eradicate the rival elite, root and branch. When Isa Vermehren,[3] who was herself a victim of *Sippenhaft* (i.e., the system of imprisonment because of kinship) arrived at Buchenwald, she met there ten Stauffenbergs, eight Goerdelers and so on. But some individuals and some families have been saved. Moreover, from a number of evidences it would appear that many, particularly among the younger generation in Germany, are trying to start a new life from the ground up, as individuals, as members of their families or of small communities. They are allergic to any kind of propaganda and want above all, as Goerdeler would have put it, "respect for truth" and "veneration for justice." In a country where the roots have been laid open in every possible sense, and where, in the words of Count Lehndorff, "every treasured possession has been forcefully torn away," it is natural that fundamental questions are taken up with an intense seriousness. And many examples could be quoted which seem to prove, that in small circles, concerned with religious, philosophical, or social problems and with doing—in a quiet way—what is necessary to do in the immediate neighborhood, the "other Germany" continues. Some observers even speak of a moral uplift in the midst of all corrupting influences. Whether these energies can withstand the sheer weight of despair and the avalanche of nihilism nobody will dare to predict.

It must suffice to state in a final comment that the German opposition has left behind ideals which are not bound up with locality or nationality. This gives to it a unique character. While the German resistance was part of a European resistance, it has some features of its own which derive from special conditions. Elsewhere among the fighters for liberation—and this is not said for the purpose of criticism—there were undoubtedly rogues, attracted by opportunities of violence suitable to their taste. In the German opposition there were none of the "underworld" elements of whom the *New York Times* spoke. Hitler could use them all. Moreover, the German opposition

---

[3] *Reise durch den letzten Akt* (Hamburg, 1947), pp. 152–53. This very interesting report gives also impressive evidences of the truly international spirit among the persecuted.

found itself in, or came gradually into, the exceptional position that to fight for liberation was to fight for defeat. The only way of solving this dilemma was to substitute a positive for a negative ideal, an ideal which transcended the struggle against the Nazis or against external oppression and which was not fulfilled with the overthrow of a regime or the removal of tyranny from just one nation. It needed stronger impulses which were basically human and at the same time of universal validity. Thus, the leading men of the German opposition were in some respects standard bearers in the midst of chaos. They were, as has been said, "much more than the mere opposites of Hitler and his accursed system; their struggle was, beyond its factual meaning for the events of our time, on a higher plane, the attempt to overcome spiritually the nineteenth century."

The Countess Marion Dönhoff[4] who wrote these words seems to sum up very aptly what was in the mind of many whose names have occurred on these pages and in particular of the Kreisau circle. She adds as a further characterization of their innermost concern: "Only one thing is important, to liberate man who has become an empty shell, a tool of techniques, a creation of abstract political ideas, a function of scientific knowledge, a servant of economic laws which he has himself made absolute—to liberate that man of all preconceptions and to erect once more before him the genuine *humanitas*, the true picture of man in his worth and his nobility. Only then, when man shall have taken his rightful place, will be fulfilled the prerequisite for harmony in the individual and thus also in the state. But this is impossible unless man once more recalls his origin and remembers his creation in the image of God and all the responsibility that this implies."

[4] "In Memoriam, 20. Juli 1944" (Hamburg).

INDEX

Abwehr. See German Intelligence Service.
Albrecht-Marburg, Professor, 101
Allied powers: negative attitude towards peace overtures, 147, 148
Almond, Gabriel A., 14, n. 10, 98, n. 115
American Committee to Aid Survivors of the German Resistance, 84, n. 79
Andreas-Friedrich, Ruth, *Berlin Underground*, 33
Anti-Nazism, 52, 85, 97
Anti-Semitism, 31, 34, 41, 42, 65
Antitotalitarianism, 43, 44, 46, 94
Aschmann, 55
Atlantic Charter, 148, 151
Atonement, 158

Bästlein, 54
Bauer, Otto, 50
Bayne, E. A., 22, n. 24
Beck, Colonel General Ludwig, 57, 58, 59, n. 31, 60–62, 68, 71, 76, 79, 83, 91, 93, 100, 101, 103, 107, 109, 123, 133, 139, 144, 146
Belgians, King of, 134
Berchtesgaden, 61
Bergengruen, Werner, 35, n. 28
Berggrav, Bishop, 115
Bernstorff, Count Albrecht von, 33, n. 23, 81
Bibelforscher, Ernste, 40
Bismarck, Herbert von, 56
Blaskowitz, General, 66, n. 39
Blomberg, Field Marshal Werner von, 64, 67, 69
Bolz, Eugen Anton, 89, 96
Bonhoeffer, Claus, 141
Bonhoeffer, Dietrich, 5, 46, 83, 101, 141, 142, n. 24, 143, 144, 146
Bormann, Martin, 92
Bosch, Robert, 54, 85, 101
Bose, Von, 52
Bramstedt, E. K., *Dictatorship and Political Police*, 27, n. 7
Brauchitsch, Field Marshal Walter von, 58, 70, n. 45, 79
Bredow, General von, 52
British Broadcasting Company, 39
British Foreign Office, 62, 144, 146
British Secret Service, 54
British *White Book. Germany No. 2* (1939), 31, n. 16
Brockdorf, General von, 59
Brockwell, R., *Central European Observer*, 13, n. 8

Brown Book of the Hitler Terror, 17
Brüning, Heinrich, 52, 56, 76, n. 57, 93, 133, 138
Buchenwald concentration camp, 18, 165
Buchholz, Father Heinz, 10, n. 3
Bülow, Bernhard von, 55, 56, 60
Burney, Christopher, *The Dungeon Democracy*, 18, n. 17
Butcher, Harry C., *My Three Years with Eisenhower*, 150
Byrnes, James F., *Speaking Frankly*, 151, n. 38

Canaris, Admiral Wilhelm, 63, 77, 81, 83, 93, n. 99, 95, 139
Carossa, Hans, 35, n. 28
Casablanca, Conference of, 149, 151, 153, 157
Central Committee (Communist) for Germany, 127
Centrists, 47, 49, 50, 54, 139
Chamberlain, Neville, 59–62, 132, 135
Chichester, Bishop of, 89, 99, 140–43
Christian solidarity, 45
Christian spirit, 116–18, 119
Christian Trade Unions, 139
Church and state, 40
Churchill, Winston, 24, 61, 63, 130–32, 151, 152
Communists, 47–50, 98, 128
Concentration camps, 13, 18, 19, 46; Germans in, 18; priests & ministers in, 42
Concordat of July 20, 1933, 40
Confessing Church, 41, 46, 65, 101, 114, 139; memorandum to Hitler (Whitsuntide, 1936), 41
Constitutional law, 105, n. 131
Corona, 35
Counter Intelligence. *See* German Intelligence Service.
Court of International Justice, 120
Czechoslovakian crisis (1938), 58–63

Dachau, 32, 42
Dachau SS, 18, n. 17
Dahrendorf, Gustav, 84, 95
Daladier, Edouard, 61, 132
Delbrück, Justus, 83
Delp, Alois, S.J., 10, 14; *Im Angesicht des Todes* 10, n. 3
Democratic party, 139
Denazification, 108, 109
Deutsch, Harold C., 82, n. 75, 149
Deutsche Rundschau, 35, 38, 39, 54

167

Dietrich, Sepp, 66, n. 39
Dietze, Constantin von, 101
Dodd, William E., 35
Dönhoff, Countess Marion, *In Memoriam 20. Juli 1944*, 71, n. 48, 166
Dohnanyi, Dr. Hans von, 83, 141
Dohna-Tolksdorf, Count, 89
Dulles, Allen Welsh, 20, 87, n. 84, 91, 95, 128, n. 169, 149, 150; *Germany's Underground*, 11 n. 5, 22
Duncan-Jones, A. S., *The Struggle for Religious Freedom in Germany*, 41, n. 39

Ebbinghaus, Julius, *Zu Deutschlands Schicksalwende*, 25, n. 4
Ebenstein, W., 13, n. 8
Eckardt, W. v., 111, n. 143
Eckert, J., *Schuldig oder Entlastet*, 30, n. 13
Economic and social planning, 109, 110, 119
Edelweiss movement, 12, n. 6, 14
Eden, Anthony, 143, 144
Einsiedel, Von, 113
Eisenhower, General Dwight D., 19, 20, 150
Elections, 17; March, 1933, 47
Elsas, Dr., 89
Elser, G., 53, 54
Enabling Act (March 23, 1933), 48
Erb, Alfons, *Bernhard Lichtenberg*, 32, n. 21
Etzdorf, Von, 55
Eucken, Walter, 101

Falkenhausen, General Alexander von, 73
Faulhaber, Cardinal, Archbishop of Munich, 41, 133
Federalism, 52, 104–7, 146, 147, 163, 164
Feiling, Keith, *Life of Neville Chamberlain*, 132, n. 8
Fellgiebel, General Erich, 73
Ford, Franklin L., 22, 59, n. 31
Fraenkel, H., *The German People versus Hitler* 32, n. 22
Frankfurter Zeitung, 38
Fraternization between Germans and Russians, 156
Free German Trade Unions, 92, 97, 139
Freisler, Roland, 126, 127
Freytag-Loringhoven, Colonel von, 73
Friedländer, Ernst, *Von der inneren Not*, 25, n. 4
Fritsch, General Werner von, 65, 69, 75
Fromm, Colonel General Fritz, 70, 74

Gaevernitz, Gero von S., 149, 153
Galen, Cardinal Count von, Bishop of Münster, 44
George, Stefan, 72
Gerard, James W., 17, 23
German air force, 63

German Air Ministry, 12, 54, 64
German army: opposed to war, 61
German Army officers, 65, 66; and Nazism, 66, 67; attitude towards resistance, 70; corruption of, 67, 68; fight the SS, 66; purge of, 69
German bishops, 41
German Books, A Selective Critical Bibliography, 37, n. 31
German Foreign Office, 32, 55, 60, 61, 115, 133, 135
German General Staff, 81, 82, 83
German Intelligence Service, 16, 64, 66, n. 38, 74, 77, n. 63, 81–83, 94, 141, 146
German Liberty party (*Deutsche Freiheitspartei*), 55
German National Socialist Workers Party, votes for, 17
German navy, 63
German opposition: Allied policy towards, 147, 148; civilians in, 83, 99, 139; difficulties for, 15, 16; ideals of, 156, 164–66; nature of, 159, 160
German youth movement (1920's), 113
Germans identified with Nazis, 132, 147, 152, 153
Germans outside Germany, Allied attitude towards, 132, n. 9
Germany: non-aggression pact with U.S.S.R., 48, 49, n. 4
Gersdorff, Von, 73, 77
Gerstenmeier, Eugen, 114, 115, 122, 125
Gessler, Otto, 89, 96, 102
Gestapo, 9, 10, 13, 14, 49, 50, 57, 64, 74, 98, 127
Gilbert, F., 36, n. 30
Gisevius, Hans Bernard, 57–59, 60, n. 32, 66, n. 38, 69, 90, 92, 126, n. 163, 128, 149, 154; *To the Bitter End*, 29, n. 12
Godesberg, 61
Goebbels, Paul Joseph, 39, 63, 82, 142, 150
Goerdeler, Carl Friedrich, 57, 60–62, 69–71, 76, 83, 85–91, 94, 95, 100–10, 120, 123–25, 131–34, 144–47, 158; "*An die Generalität*," 87; *Politisches Testament*, 61, n. 34; "Primer of Economics," 100
Goerdeler, Frau, 57, n. 26, 85, n. 80, 100
Göring, Hermann Wilhelm, 39, 91, 142
Goetze-Jena, Dr., 101
Gollancz, Victor, 18, 152; *Our Threatened Values*, 18, n. 17
Great Britain, 146, 147
Green Reports, 50, n. 7
Grimme, Ad., 13, n. 7
Gross, Nikolaus, 94
Gurian, Waldemar, *Antisemitism in Modern Germany*, 31, n. 15
Guttenberg, Baron Karl Ludwig von, 83

Habermann, Max, 94
Haecker, Th., 12
Haeften, Johannes Bernd von, 115
Haeften, Lieutenant Werner von, 115
Halder, General Franz, 57, n. 28, 59, 60, n. 32, 61–63, 70, n. 45, 79, 82
Halem, Von, 53, 54
Halifax, Viscount, 60, 62, 130
Hamm, 90
Hammerstein-Equord, Colonel General Kurt von, 59, n. 31, 64, 66, n. 38, 67, 70, 76, 93, 94, 103
Hardenberg, Count von, 73
Harnack, Arvid, 12, 13, n. 7, 54
Harnack, Axel von, 13, n. 7
Harnack, Ernst von, 54, 95
Hase, Lieutenant General Paul von, 73
Hassell, Ulrich von, 62, 69, 70, 72, 83, 87–90, 93, 96, 100–3, 109, 123, 132, 133, 144; *Diaries*, 87, n. 84; *Vom anderen Deutschland*, 102, n. 122
Haubach, Theodor, 95, 96, 114, 123, 124
Hauptmann, Gerhart, 35, n. 28
Hausen, Colonel Georg, 73
Haushofer, Albrecht, 135; "Moabiter Sonnette," *ibid*.
Haushofer, Dr. Heinz, 135, n. 14
Heisenberg, Professor, 72
Helldorff, Count Wolf Heinrich von, 29, n. 12, 59
Henderson, Sir Neville, 63, n. 35
Henk, Emil, 83, n. 77, 99
Hermes, Andreas, 54, 89
Heuss, Theodor, *Robert Bosch*, 85, n. 80
Heussinger, Lieutenant General Adolf, 73
Hilferding, Rudolf, 90
Himmler, Heinrich, 54, 91, 142, n. 23
Hindenburg, Paul von, 64
Hitler, Adolf, 20, 24, 59, 61, 64, 66, n. 39, 68, 80, 82, 130–32, 136, 152, 156; oath to, 67, 68; plots against, 53, 54, 59, 75–78
Hitler Youth, 14, 67
Hoare, Sir Samuel, *Complacent Dictator*, 81, n. 72
Hochland, 12, 35
Hoeppner, Colonel General Erich, 59
Hofacker, Lieutenant Colonel Caesar von, 74, n. 53
Hoffmann, Wilhelm, *Nach der Katastrophe*, 36, n. 29
Huber, Kurt, 12
Huch, Ricarda, 35, n. 28
Hugenberg, Alfred, 52, 89
Husen, P. van, "The 20th of July and the German Catholics," 45, n. 49, 114

Inner Emigration, 14
Inside Germany Reports, 50, n. 6

Intellectual life, 36–38
Intellectuals: opposition to Nazism, 35; responsibility for Nazism, 34–35
International Labor Organization, 92
Internationalism, 146, 147, 163

Jacob, Franz, 54
Jansen, J. B. & St. Weyl, *The Silent War*, 13, n. 9
Jaspers, Karl, *Die Schuldfrage*, 25
Jessen, Jens Peter, 72, 102, 123
Joos, Joseph, *Leben auf Widerruf*, 19, n. 18
Juenger, Ernst, *On the Marble Cliffs*, 39
Juenger, Fr. Georg, 35, n. 28
Jung, Edgar J., 51, 52; *The Rule of the Inferiors*, 52

Kaiser, Hermann, 70, 74, n. 54, 83, 101
Kaiser, Jakob, 54, 83, 94, 96, 98, 100, 105, 106, 140
Kaiser, Ludwig, 70, n. 42, 83
Kapp putsch, 48, 103
Keitel, Field Marshal Wilhelm, 69
Kempner, Dr., 33, n. 23
Kessel, Albrecht von, 56
Kiep, Otto C., 32, 56, 127
Kirk, Alexander, 133, 134
Klausener, 52
Kleist, Ewald von, 53, 73, 89
Kleist, Heinrich von, 38
Kluge, Field Marshal Günther von, 70, 71, 77
Knappen, M., *And Call it Peace*, 27, n. 6
Koerner, Heinrich, 94
Kogon, E., *Der SS-Staat*, 13, n. 8, 18, n. 17, 19, n. 18
Kollontay, Mme. Alexandra Michailovna, 154
Kordt, Dr. Erich, 56, 60, 62, 132; *Wahn und Wirklichkeit*, 56, n. 23
Kordt, Theodor, 60, 62
Krause, Friedrich, 62, n. 34
Kreisau circle, 45, 56, 72, 90, 95, 103, 109, 111–29, 146, 155; Christian spirit in, 116–18, 123; educational ideas of, 118; principles of, 117
Kuenzer, Richard, 33, n. 23

Lahousen, Major General, 81, n. 72
Lampe, Adolf, 101
Langbehn, Dr. Carl, 83, 91, 92, 103, n. 127
Leber, Julius, 95, 96, 98, 124, 127, 128, 135
Lehndorff, Count von, 73, 80
Lehr, Dr., 89
Lejeune-Jung, Paul, 89, 96
Lend, Evelyn, *The Underground Struggle in Germany*, 47, n. 2
Letterhaus, Bernhard, 94, 96
Leuninger, Franz, 94

Leuschner, Wilhelm, 92, 93, 96, 98–100, 106, 135
Ley, Dr. Robert, 27, 66
Lichtenberg, Msgr. Bernhard, 32
Lindemann, 73
Litt-Leipzig, Professor, 101
Lochner, Louis P., 71, n. 47, 138, 140, 144
Loeser, Ewald, 96
Loewenstein, Karl, 97, n. 111
London, missions to, 60, 62
Louis Ferdinand, 103
Lüninck, Baron von, 89, 96
Lukaschek, Hans, 114
Lutheranism, 40

Maas, Hermann, 93
Macartney, C. A., *National State and National Minorities*, 146, n. 29
Maerker, Paul, 97
Maley, Alexander B., 22, 136, nn. 17 & 18, 138
Mann, Thomas, 37, n. 32
Markwitz, 54
Marsh, Ellen, *The Silent War*, 14, n. 11
Martin, Hugh, *Christian Counter-Attack*, 41, n. 39
Mayer, Carl, 40, n. 38
Meier, J. A., *Geflüstertes*, 28, n. 8
Meinecke, Friedrich, *Die deutsche Katastrophe*, 25, n. 4, 71, n. 48
Mennonites, 40
Michel, Karl, *Ost und West*, 72, n. 49, 129, n. 170
Micklem, N., *National Socialism and Christianity*, 41, n. 39; *National Socialism and the Roman Catholic Church*, ibid.
Mierendorff, Carlo, 95, 114, 123
Mischler, Dr., 54
"Moabiter Sonnette," 135
Molo, Walter v., 35, n. 28
Moltke, Countess Freya von, 112, n. 145, 124, n. 160, 125, 126
Moltke, Count Helmuth Jakob von, 11, 28, 112, 115–21, 125–27; *A German of the Resistance*, 11, n. 4
Monarchy, 103
Morgenthau, 19, 20
Morgenthau plan, 151
Morley, Felix, 136
Muckermann, Father Friedrich, *Der deutsche Weg*, 45, n. 49
Müller, Heinrich "Gestapo," 49, n. 4
Müller, Joseph, 89, 133
Müller, Ludwig, Reichsbischof, 44, 94
Müller, Wolfgang, *Gegen eine neue Dolchstosslegende*, 75, n. 55
Mumm, Herbert v., 33, n. 23
Muncy, Lysbeth W., "The Junkers, etc.," 89, n. 90

Munich agreement, 61, 62
Munich *Reichswehr*, 64
Munich student manifesto (Feb. 18, 1943), 12
Munich student revolt (Feb., 1943), 11, 12
Münsterland, "Popular revolt" in, 44
Mussolini, Benito, 28, 61

Nazi Conspiracy and Aggression, 31, n. 20
Nazi opponents, 29
Nazi system, 24
Nazis, 48
Nazism and religion, 41
Nebe, Artur, 66, n. 38, 29, n. 12
Neuerscheinungen der deutschen wissenschaftlichen Literatur, 1939–1945, 37, n. 31
"New Beginners," 49
New Beginning—A Secret German Manifesto, 49
Nicolson, Arthur, 32, n. 23
Niekisch, *Hitler, a German Disaster*, 53
Niemöller, Martin, 43, 44, n. 45, 103, n. 127
Norwegian Underground, 114, 115
"Nuremberg laws," 65, n. 37

OKW (*Oberkommando der Wehrmacht*, Supreme Command of the Armed Forces), 69, 73
Olbricht, General Friedrich, 70, n. 42, 71, 73, 77, 93, 96
Opposition propaganda, 50, 51
OSS (Office of Strategic Services), 20
Oster, Major General Hans, 81, 90, 96, 141
OWI (Office of War Information), 20, 152

Paetel, K. O. *Deutsche Innere Emigration*, 33, n. 23
Papen, Franz von, 51, 52
Pechel, Rudolf, 39, 45, 52, 54, 59, n. 31, 62, 76; *Deutscher Widerstand*, 11, n. 5
People's Court (*Volksgerichtshof*), 89, 126
Perels, 89
Picard, Max, *Hitler in Our Selves*, 23
Planck, Erwin, 90, 93, 157
Ploetzensee, 10, n. 3
Pölchau, Harald, Lutheran chaplain, 10, 11, n. 4, 114
Poland, 144, 145
Political parties, outlawing of, 48
Political reorganization, proposed, 96, 101–7, 121–22, 142
Popitz, Johannes, 72, 90–92, 100, 101, 102, 103, n. 127, 105, n. 131, 109, 123
Powers, Michael, *Religion in the Third Reich*, 41, n. 39
Preysing, Cardinal Count von, Archbishop of Berlin, 45, 85
Prisoners, political, 13, 14, 98
"Protective corps," 19
Protestant clergy, executions of, 44

Protestantism, 40, 45
"Prussianism," 63, 64, 71, 82
Purges, 52, 69
Puttkamer, Von, 89

Quakers, 40
Quebec agreement (September, 1944), 151
Quirnheim, Colonel Merz von, 73

Racial legislation, 65
Reichenau, General Walter von, 64, 66, n. 39
Reichstag fire, 48
Reichswehr, 64, 65, n. 37, 67; their oath to Hitler, 67, 68
Reichwein, Adolf, 95, 114, 115, 127
Religious persecution, 41, 44, 98
Resistance (Widerstand), 53
Reusch, 54
Reuter, Franz, *Der 20. Juli*, 157, n. 49
Ribbentrop, Joachim von, 56, 90
Ribbentrop Bureau, 56
Riezler, Kurt, 23, n. 2
Ritter, Gerhard, 15, n. 12, 101
Röhm, Ernst, 67
Röhm-putsch, 51
Roemer circle, 53
Roenne, Von, 73
Röpke, W., *Die deutsche Frage*, 14, n. 10
Roesch, Father, S. J., 114
Rommel, Field Marshal Erwin, 70
Roosevelt, Franklin D., 138, 140, 151
Rosenberger, H., *Wehrmachtsrechtsabteilung*, 69
Rote Kapelle, 12, 13, n. 7, 54
Rothfels, Hans, "The Baltic Provinces," 146, n. 29; "Frontiers and Mass Migrations," *ibid.*
Rupprecht, 103
Russia. *See* U.S.S.R.

SA (*Sturmabteilung*, Storm Troopers), 51, 67
Sack, Dr. Carl, 83
Saefkow, Anton, 54
St. Annaberg, pilgrimage to, 40, n. 46
Salin, Edgar, 78, n. 66, 124, n. 160, 126, n. 163
Sarre, Marie-Louise, 91
Sas, Colonel G. J., 82, n. 74
Schacht, Dr. Hjalmar, 57, 60, 90, 92
Schlabrendorff, Fabian von, 10, n. 1, 53, 62, 63, n. 35, 69, 73, n. 52, 132; *Offiziere gegen Hitler*, 54, n. 19; *They Almost Killed Hitler*, 10, n. 1, 21
Schleicher, General Kurt von, 52, 65
Schleicher, Dr. Rüdiger, 83, 141
Schmidt, Dr. Paul, 55
Schmitt, Dr., 94
Schneider, Reinhold, 25, 26, 35, n. 28; *Das Unzerstörbare*, 26, n. 5
Schneppenhorst, Ernst, 93

Schönfeld, Dr. Hans, 140, 141, n. 21, 142, 143
Scholarship, 36
Scholl, Hans, 12
Scholl, Sophie, 12
Scholz, Wilhelm v., 35, n. 28
Schroeder, Rudolf A., 35, n. 28
Schütz, W., *German Home Front*, 36, n. 29, *Pens under the Swastika, ibid.*
Schulenburg, Count Fritz von der, 115
Schulenburg, Count Werner von der, 89, 96, 154
Schulze-Boysen, Harold, 13, 54
Schwamb, Ludwig, 94
Schwerin-Schwanenfeld, Count Ulrich von, 83, 115
Shirer, William L., 37, n. 32, 54, 139
Shulman, Major Milton, *Defeat in the West*, 82
Silens, Constantin, *Irrweg und Umkehr*, 59, n. 30
Smend, Rudolf, 101
Social Democratic party, 47, 48, 50, 93, 139
Socialists, 47, 49, 54, 98
Solf, Frau Hanna, 32, 33
Solf-Kreis, 32
Soviet Union. *See* U.S.S.R.
Soviets, 12
Speer, Albert, 29, n. 11
Speidel, Lieutenant General Hans, 74
SS (*Schutzstaffel*), 19, 51, 57, 64, 66, 67, 74, 75
Stalin, Joseph, 154
"Mr. Stallforth," 134, 145, n. 27
Stauffenberg, Colonel Count Claus Schenk von, 72, 76-78, 96, 126, n. 163, 127, 128, 156
Stein, Baron vom, 105
Steltzer, Theodor, 56, 96, 114, 115
Stieff, Major General Helmuth, 73
Struenk, Theodor, 83, 149
Stülpnagel, General Count Heinrich von, 73, 74
Stuttgart declaration, 43
Sudeten, 145
Sulzberger, C. L., 59, n. 31
Supreme Command of the Armed Forces. *See* OKW
Swing, Raymond G., 150, 151

Tassigny, General de Lattre de, 19
Teheran, Conference of, 151
Tellenbach, Gerd, *Die deutsche Not als Schuld und Schicksal*, 25, n. 4
Thadden, Frau Ehrengard Schramm-von, 33, n. 23
Thadden, Elisabeth von, 32
They Fought Hitler First, 13, n. 8
Thomas, General Georg, 79
Thompson, Dorothy, 33, n. 23, 132, n. 9
Throtha, Von, 113

171

Trade Unionists, 98
Tresckow, Major General Henning von, 73, 77, 79, 80, 125
Treviranus, 52
Trevor-Roper, H. R., *The Last Days of Hitler*, 15, n. 12
Trott zu Solz, Adam von, 62, 115, 132, 135–39, 144–46, 149, 154, 155; *Heinrich v. Kleist*, 38
Twardowski, Von, 55
Twentieth of July, 9, 10, 20, 21, 69, 73, 84, 152; in Paris, 74

"Unconditional surrender," 149–57
U.S.S.R., 153, 154; non-aggression pact with Germany, 48, 49, n. 4
United States, 61, 137–39, 146, 147
U.S. Department of State, 136

Vagts, A., 19, n. 18
Vansittart, 132
Vatican, 40, 133
Vermehren, Isa, *Reise durch den letzten Akt*, 165, n. 3
Versailles Treaty, 145
Vossler, Karl, *Gedenkrede für die Opfer an der Universität München*, 11, n. 5

Waetjen, Eduard, 91, n. 94, 149
Wagner, General Edouard, 73
Wallenbergs, The (Jakob, Marc, Marcus, Sr.), 134
War Ministry, 56, 61, 65, 66
Weber, Alfred, 98

Weimar Republic, 47, 52
Weinreich, M., *Hitler's Professors*, 35, n. 27
Weisse Blätter, 35
Weizsäcker, Baron Ernst von, 60, 146
Wells, Sumner, 132, 134, 138, n. 19
Weltlinger (Berlin City Council), 33
Wenzel-Teutschental, 89
"White Rose," Letters of, 12
Wiechert, Ernst, 35, n. 28, 39, 45; *The Forest of the Dead*, 39, n. 37; *The Poet and His Time*, ibid.
Wilhelm, ex-Crown Prince, 103
Wilson, Sir Horace, 61
Wirmer, Dr. Joseph, 89, 96, 139
Wirth, Joseph, 133
Witzleben, Field Marshal Erwin von, 59, 73, 75, 76, 96, 107, n. 135, 146
Wolf, Eric, 101
World Council of Churches, 140
"World Peace Program," Goerdeler's, 146, 147
Wurm, Protestant Bishop of Würtemberg, 85

Yorck, Marion, 112, n. 145, 124, n. 160
Yorck von Wartenburg, Count Peter, 72, 112, 117, 125, 127

Zarden, Dr., 33, n. 23
Zeitzler, 79
Zink, H., *American Military Government in Germany*, 27, n. 6
Zitzewitz, Von, 89
Zuckmayer, Carl, *Des Teufels General*, 53, n. 13